RAISING READERS

Members of the Committee include:

Dr. Julie M. T. Chan—California State University, Long Beach

Dr. Vivian E. L. Cox—University of Arizona

Dr. Joan I. Glazer—Rhode Island College

Dr. Mary B. Howard—University of Alabama

Dr. Jane B. Mantanzo—Educational Consultant, Damascus, Maryland

Dr. Miken Olson—Brigham Young University

Ms. Betsy Rosen—University of Illinois

Dr. Marilou Sorensen—University of Utah

Dr. Evelyn Wenzel—University of Florida

Ms. Liz Wildberger—Prince George's County Schools, Librarian

Dr. Linda Leonard Lamme—University of Florida, Chair

RAISING READERS

A Guide to Sharing Literature with Young Children

The National Council of Teachers
of English,
by its Committee on Literature in the
Elementary Language Arts

Linda Leonard Lamme
with Vivian Cox,
Jane Matanzo and
Miken Olson

WALKER AND COMPANY • New York

The authors are grateful to the following publishers for permission to quote from their works:

The University of California Press for the quotation on page xviii-xix from *From Two to Five* by Kornei Chukovsky, copyright © 1963.

The Viking Press, for the quotation on page 29 from *Bequest of Wings: A Family's Pleasures with Books*, by Annis Duff, copyright © 1944.

The quotation on page 82 is reprinted by permission of the American Library Association from *Let's Read Together*, pp. vii-viii, copyright © 1964 by the American Library Association.

On page 117-118, from *Winnie-the-Pooh* by A. A. Milne, copyright © 1926, by E. P. Dutton; renewal © 1954 by A. A. Milne. Reprinted by permission of the publishers, E. P. Dutton.

First published in the United States of America in 1980 by the
Walker Publishing Company, Inc.

Published simultaneously in Canada by Beaverbooks,
Limited, Pickering, Ontario.

ISBN: 0-8027-0654-1

Library of Congress Catalog Card Number: 80-80454

Printed in the United States of America

10 9 8 7 6 5 4 3 2 1

Contents

IV: *Sharing Literature with Your Beginning Reader* 108

V: *Summary and What Next?* 173

Preface

This book is the culmination of a charge by the National Council of Teachers of English to its Committee on Literature in the Elementary Language Arts to prepare a publication for parents "to help them know good literature for children and ways to share literature with their children."

The members of the literature committee met in November of 1977 to organize the project. Between that time and June of 1978 a first draft of the material was prepared. From June 1978 to June 1979 the book was reviewed by each member of the committee, by five parents, and by the Editorial Board of NCTE. These revisions were incorporated into the present book.

However, since the manuscript was reviewed by so many individuals we view the end product as a joint effort. The Editorial Board of the National Council of Teachers of English has endorsed the book. For that endorsement, we are grateful.

Introduction

The purpose of this book is to share with parents—and others—a variety of ideas for getting young children involved with literature from infancy until the beginning reading stages. Our purpose is not to encourage the direct teaching of reading—although children who are involved with books from a very early age often learn to read early. Rather, we intend to show how both children and their parents can find enjoyment in experiencing literature.

We hope that as you read this book you'll get some ideas for making literature part of your children's lives. For each age level—infants, toddlers, prereaders, and beginning readers—we will:

recommend specific books*
share ideas for reading aloud
share ideas for your home reading environment
share ideas for family reading habits
share ideas for library reading habits
share ideas for involving your child with literature.

If you are interested in helping your baby or young child
learn to love books and develop the reading habit, this
book is for you.

---

*Inevitably some of the books we recommend will become unavailable at
bookstores or from the publishers, but most of them should remain available
from local public libraries.

Two Warnings

You will find both on the checklists and in the chapters that follow many, many ideas and suggestions. No parent could ever do everything that is recommended—nor should. Don't kill literature by pushing it on your child. One or two activities related to any one book is enough. Our premise is that a parent with lots of ideas for involving the young child with literature is more likely to be able to match the child's needs than the parent with one idea.

Second, forget about teaching your child to read. Just enjoy literature with her.* The reading will come naturally as she becomes ready. Use the ideas and suggestions that sound good to you and that come naturally. Don't push your child into reading.

*As is often the case, our language is lagging behind changes that are taking place in society, and there has been as yet no satisfactory way devised to give equal weight to the sexes when using indeterminate personal pronouns. Rather than interrupt the flow of the text by saying "s/he," "she/he," or "she or he" each time we refer back to the word "child," we have elected to alternate the use of "she" and "he" as the least of several evils.

Perspectives

Ours is a print-oriented society; books of many types are abundantly available. Hence, it is a natural part of our child-rearing practices to introduce the young child to books very early. We introduce them for pleasure, not instruction. Early in a child's life, literature can be shared as a way of saying, "I love you."

The book shared, the story told, the verse recited— each provides a pleasurable experience as basic to your child's development as more obvious kinds of nourishment. Marvelous things happen as spin-offs of warm, sharing experiences with books. Zena Sutherland and May Hill Arbuthnot, two experts on children's literature, have written: "Books are not substitute for living, but they can add immeasurably to its richness. . . . This is as true for children as for adults."[1]

Equally important, parents find that when they share literature with their young children, they, as adults, also reap many rewards. They may discover, or rediscover, that many books for even very young toddlers have an appeal for all ages. Sharing a story with a baby or young child is an opportunity for cuddling, as satisfying for the parent as for the little one. And as youngsters begin to identify with the characters in books, to sing songs and chant nursery rhymes, to recognize words and learn to read, the shared moments with literature become precious experiences for both parents and children.

What do we know about the child's literary needs? How does the child develop a sense of literature? We believe the answers to these two questions are basic for bringing children and books together. A number of publications for parents give advice on raising children, but few of these deal directly with bringing literary experiences to very young children. This book has been developed as our attempt to correct this omission and to provide parents with a comfortable starting point for sharing rewarding literary experiences with their children.

The love affair between children and books should begin early in life. Literature is your resource; how you use it may well help determine your child's reading attitudes and habits for the rest of his or her life.

What Do We Know about the Literary Needs of Children?

One of the young child's most critical literary needs is a literary model—a person she cares about who clearly loves literature. In the earliest years that model is usually a parent. How important it is for the child to see parents as people who care about literature! And there are many ways to demonstrate a love of books. Have a variety of books in your home—and use them. Trips to the library, browsing in book stores, talking to your child about stories and books, and telling stories and reading books to your children are all ways to show you care for literature. Take your child to a neighborhood story hour, have family read-aloud periods at home, meet with any authors who may live in your community, make simple books about some experiences your child has recently had.

Continuous exposure to books, beginning in infancy, is another important literary need of young children. Literature has so many facets that the question for parents becomes not when to begin, but how. What is your child like? What can he do? What does he encounter in the course of his day? At every point in the child's development, literary options are available which are in harmony with developmental rhythms. Matching your child with the perfect book will become an exciting mental game for you.

Let us give some examples. In the infant chapter you'll read that the tiny infant will calm down when listening to you read aloud from an adult magazine, but that later, as she begins reaching out with her hands, you can "match" her level by providing books that are good for pointing and page turning. The toddler chapter will suggest giving your child tiny "portable" editions to carry around with him. Ways to encourage your child to "read" by memorizing a story will appear in the prereader chapter. And you'll learn how to encourage rather than correct your beginning reader. In each chapter the developmental progress of your child is matched to books and to experiences with literature.

How Does Your Child Develop a Sense of Literature?

A sense of literature develops over a long period of time; it is not an instant product of a few experiences. Repeated experiences with books will give your child critical information in two areas: (1) language awareness and (2) literary awareness. Together these processes are called "metalinguistic awareness" by professionals. Have you ever seen a child point to a sign and say, "E-S-S-O spells gas!"? That child is aware that what is written on the sign must communicate meaning. Similarly, the prereading child who has memorized the story and corrects you while you are reading it aloud really understands the meaning of a "story." This kind of awareness develops as a result of a child's active participation in reading experiences. In addition, experiences with literature that encourage the child's active participation lead to the development of reading and storytelling habits that will pay dividends throughout life. A sense of literature is acquired through encounters with both oral and written language.

One early childhood educator described this process when he wrote: ". . . although each new generation of parents, grandfathers, and grandmothers sings and recites to children both the good and the inferior, only that which best serves the children's needs and tastes remains in their memories. And when he reaches old age, everyone who heard in his childhood these folk chants passes on to his grandchildren, in turn, the very best, the most vivid and vital. And everything that is out of tune and incongruous with the psychology of the young child is gradually forgotten and becomes extinct; . . . In this way an exemplary children's folklore has come into existence—exemplary in its language and rhythm, as well as ideally suited to the intellectual needs of the young child."[2]

Poets and authors are linguistic magicians; they perform magic with language. Their work provides language models for your child. Book language is not the same as oral language or television language. People don't talk like books! You probably tend to simplify your speech when you are talking to your infant, toddler, or young child. Young children have many experiences with language, but in a television society and one in which often both parents are away all day working, the adults must make a special effort to provide their children with opportunities to listen to books. As Leland B. Jacobs, a college professor and author of books for children said: "Literature is beautiful language, and who among us does not want children to get the beauty of their tongue at its best?"[3]

Guidelines to Use in Determining Literary Experiences for Your Child

In your effort to involve your children with books it is important that you capitalize upon opportunities to share literature with them. Bedtime has traditionally been the time when parents read to their children. In addition, any time that a story or poem fits a real-life situation is an excellent time for book sharing. Keep in mind that sharing books with children is a natural activity and should be an extension of experiences that are a natural part of the day.

Also remember that your child's experience with books should be pleasurable. Share those stories and poems that *you* enjoy. You'll find that these sessions with books quickly become special treats for the child.

Fictional characters will come alive for him and he will beg you to read favorite stories over and over again.

How long a literary session should last is another thing to consider. It can be anywhere from several seconds to many minutes, depending upon the function and the context in which the experience occurs. "Lap" stories and bedtime stories are usually of longer duration than those that occur in the bath or the kitchen. Finger plays and poems by their very nature are less time consuming than stories. Just read as long as both you and your child are enjoying the story.

"Try for variety" is a guideline of importance in the process of bringing books and children together. You'll want to expose your child to different types of books—stories, songs, workbooks, poems, homemade books, library books, hardbacks, paperbacks, etc. In doing this you'll come across many different kinds of illustrations—paintings, woodcuts, photographs, lithographs, sketches, collages, etc. Since books are likely to be one of the few encounters your child has with works of art, you'll want to be sure you share books that use a variety of types of illustration.

The content of books should concern you. Seek out books that depict unfamiliar as well as familiar events; choose books that present the kind of language and behavior you'd like your child to show. For example, Laurel, a toddler who is normally an eager eater, had been reading a book with a character in it who did not eat his supper. That evening she proudly declared, "Laurel does not eat her supper." After a week of such behavior, the book was put on a high shelf, to be brought back down in a year or so when the humor in the situation can be appreciated. Remember also that your child's encounters with book characters of other cultures and races are likely to make an impression. Avoid stereotypes and seek out strong characters regardless of their culture.

Before You Begin

Before you turn to the chapter that deals with your child's age level, take a moment to consider where you are in the important areas which follow. Then, as you proceed to gather ideas in chapters I through IV, periodically return to this section and assess your progress. Undoubtedly you'll find some areas in which you are doing a fine job. You'll also likely decide you want to improve in one area or another. Remember, no parent does everything suggested in this volume. But as you become aware of the role of literature in your young child's experience, you'll probably want to involve your child more with books. We wrote this book to help you do that.

WHERE ARE YOU NOW?

Knowledge of Literature

1. Do you know lots of books your
   child might enjoy?   Yes   No   Some
2. Do you know different kinds of
   books?   Yes   No   Some
3. Do you know books with different
   types of illustrations?   Yes   No   Some
4. Can you judge which books are
   good for your child and which
   ones aren't?   Yes   No   Sometimes
5. Are you familiar with the authors
   and illustrators of children's
   books?   Yes   No   Some

Reading Aloud

1. Before reading a book do you talk
   about it with your child?   Yes   No   Sometimes
2. Do you point to the words in the
   title as you read it?   Yes   No   Sometimes
3. Do you get your child to turn the
   pages when possible?   Yes   No   Sometimes
4. Do you point to things in pictures
   and name them?   Yes   No   Sometimes
5. Do you point to words and move
   your finger from left to right?   Yes   No   Sometimes
6. Do you read with expression in
   your voice?   Yes   No   Sometimes
7. Do you change voices for different
   characters?   Yes   No   Sometimes
8. Do you encourage your child to
   participate in the story by:

   a. Stopping and letting your child
      supply a rhyming word?   Yes   No   Sometimes
   b. Reading repetitious parts so
      that your child can join in?   Yes   No   Sometimes
   c. Giving your child lots of time to
      answer questions that you ask?   Yes   No   Sometimes
9. Do you read in a soft, pleasant
   sounding voice?   Yes   No   Sometimes
10. Do you read in different places
    around the house?   Yes   No   Sometimes
11. Do you read at different times
    during the day?   Yes   No   Sometimes
12. Can your child see the pictures as
    you read?   Yes   No   Sometimes
13. After reading the book do you talk
    about it together?   Yes   No   Sometimes
14. Do you ask questions about the
    story that have more than one
    answer (thought questions)?   Yes   No   Sometimes
15. Do you really enjoy reading with
    your child   Yes   No   Sometimes

16. Do you try to keep interruptions to
a minimum while you are reading
aloud?   Yes   No   Sometimes

Home Reading Environment
Does your home environment encourage family members to
read? (Probably no home has all these advantages, but as you
step back and observe your own home you may find a few
changes you'd like to make.)

1. Does your home include:
   a. Quiet, well-lit places for
      reading?   Yes   No
   b. Books on bookshelves or in
      boxes that children can reach?   Yes   No
   c. Magazines for children?   Yes   No
   d. Magazines and newspapers for
      adults?   Yes   No
   e. Reading materials all over the
      house—not just in one room?   Yes   No
   f. A special place to keep library
      books?   Yes   No
   g. A table where your child can
      draw and write when he wants
      to?
2. Is there a scheduled quiet time
   for reading?   Yes   No
3. Does someone in the family read
   aloud with each child in the
   family *every* day, either reading
   to a child or listening to her read? Yes   No   Sometimes
4. Do you give books as presents?   Yes   No   Sometimes
5. Do your children see adults in the
   family reading regularly?   Yes   No   Sometimes
6. Do you monitor your children's
   television viewing?   Yes   No   Sometimes
   a. Are you aware of what
      programs the children watch?   Yes   No   Sometimes

    b. Do you restrict the amount of
       time spent watching
       television?   Yes   No   Sometimes
    c. Do you restrict the shows your
       child may watch?   Yes   No   Sometimes
    d. Do you watch television with
       your child (if your child is a
       television viewer)?   Yes   No   Sometimes
7. Do you and your child attend
   book fairs?   Yes   No   Sometimes
8. Does your child participate in
   practical "reading" activities,
   such as reading signs, labels on
   foods, etc.?   Yes   No   Sometimes

Family Reading Habits
1. Do all members of your family
   read?   Yes   No   Sometimes
2. Do all members of your family
   discuss what they are reading?   Yes   No   Sometimes

Library Reading Habits
1. Do you visit the public library (or
   bookmobile) on a regular basis?   Yes   No   Sometimes
2. Does your child attend library
   story hours?   Yes   No   Sometimes
3. Do you suggest books, programs,
   or activities to members of the
   library staff?   Yes   No   Sometimes

Literature Involvement
1. Does your child have a
   flannelboard with story
   characters to use in telling
   stories?   Yes   No
2. Does your child have puppet
   characters for the stories he
   knows?   Yes   No

3. Does your child act out stories
   that have been read to her?   Yes   No   Sometimes
4. Does your child look at books
   independently?   Yes   No   Sometimes
5. Does your child pretend to read? Yes No Sometimes

Notes

[1]Zena Sutherland, and May Hill Arbuthnot, *Children and Books*, 4th ed. (Chicago: Scott, Foresman, 1972) p. 2

[2]Kornei Chukovsky, *From Two to Five*, (Berkeley and Los Angeles: University of California Press, 1963) p. 94

[3]Leland B. Jacobs, ed. *Using Literature with Young Children*. (New York: Teachers College Press, 1965)

I

Sharing Literature with Your Infant

Newborn to 1 year old

The first year of life is a critical one in the child's development, and the recent publication of so many books for parents of infants suggests that parents are turning more and more to books for advice. Many parents do not consider introducing their children to literature until the youngsters are toddlers or older, and some professional publications make no mention of infants. At least one book suggests that storytelling and reading aloud should begin during the child's second year.

The idea of sharing literature with infants, however, is not new. One can find books from a number of years back that suggest to parents that they read, talk, and sing to their infants regularly. May Becker in 1936 claimed, ". . . it seems to me that one has not had all his rights if he has not floated into consciousness to the sound of his

mother's voice, singing."[1] In the early 1940's the children's book editor, Annis Duff, wrote a whole book, *Bequest of Wings*, about her family's pleasures with
reading—infants included. In her home, books fell into
the category of pleasant necessities, "along with food,
sleep, music and all out-of-doors."[2]

More recently Nancy Larrick, the author of the peren-
nial favorite, *A Parent's Guide to Children's Reading*,
has written, "The time to begin is with the first feeding,
pampering, and bathing, when the parent's singing or
chanting and gentle conversation begin to set the stage
for the infant's participation only a few months later."[3]

There are many reasons for sharing books with
infants—even newborn infants. The first year of life is
now generally recognized as the most important forma-
tive year in the development of receptive language (listening). Your infant is beginning to respond to sounds
even before birth, and long before he can talk he is recording them. Reading aloud provides variety in the language your baby hears, since "book talk" differs greatly
from "people talk" (especially when people are talking
to infants).

Reading aloud with your infant can provide a pleasant,
relaxing interchange, just as a feeding does. Infants like
to be cuddled and rocked and it is helpful if they associate reading with this warm, physical encounter.

Infants thrive on routine. If reading becomes part of
their normal daily routine, books become an accepted
part of their world and reading time is anticipated with
joy.

Sharing books with your infant builds some very basic
reading readiness skills. Through the toddler and preschool years these accumulate to help her when she begins learning to read. Forty years ago May L. Becker
wrote, "Little as he is, long before he can be
a reader or even a listener to books, he is savoring

the first joyous mysteries of reading—recognition."[4]
Every time your baby points to "dat" he is learning to
recognize objects.

Before the age of one year, an infant who is read to
regularly begins to discover that books have pictures and
words; that there is a "right side up" to books and pictures; that pages turn and stories have a sequence; that
language has many different sounds, tones, and volumes; that pictures have meaning; and that being read to
is a comfortable way to get attention.

A final reason for reading with your infant is that *you*
will enjoy it—so much, indeed, that you will not want to
stop. You need the calm, quiet relaxation with your baby
that sharing books provides. There is great joy in reading
to your infant, in singing, chanting, and playing with her.
As May Becker noted, "I have said that a baby misses
something if he has not heard, before he knew it, his
mother singing—but I know from experience that his
mother will have missed even more."[5]

What Is Good Literature for an Infant?

Books for infants should provide opportunities to involve the child—either through language or through
touching. Pictures should be colorful, clear, and uncluttered. With a newborn, the *sound* of language is the most
important element in literature. You can read your own
adult literature aloud to the newborn; let the baby hear
you read something that you genuinely enjoy. Sing to
him. The warm feeling of being held, plus the melodic
sound of your voice, is likely to make the infant feel
loved. One parent claims that even reading to oneself
while holding your infant has some benefit.

As the infant gets older (2–4 months), but is still not

focusing on pictures, begin reading some poetry, nursery rhymes, songs or stories that have a refrain—any literature that sounds melodic. Make up stories of your own with lots of repetition, or tell familiar stories in your own words as you hold or rock you child.

As soon as the infant begins to focus on pictures, you will want to provide visual variety in the books you read to her. For the newborn to the six-month-old child, stories with colorful illustrations and with pictures of faces are appropriate. From the very start infants like to look at faces.

As the child begins to reach out to touch things you will want to introduce the "Touch and Feel" textured books listed in the annotated bibliography. From about age 8 to 14 months, provide some books that have stiff, cardboard pages that can withstand punishment from an infant's exploring fingers. If you read paperbacks bring them out only when the baby's grabbing urge is not at its height and turn the pages quickly so that they are less likely to be grabbed and torn. Books with pop-out figures are probably best suited for infants 1 to 6 months old and for those over 24 months, since the very young infant is less able to tear pages, and the two-year-old can usually understand why he is not to grab the pop-outs.

When your infant begins to experiment with sounds of her own, it's a good time for books with sounds for the child to copy, such as animal noises. For an older infant you will want books that have clear illustrations and easily identifiable people and objects for "point and say" reading sessions. Select books that reflect the child's own experience—books about animals, family members, pets, food, cars, trucks, and airplanes.

You will want to continue to read and reread all the earlier types of books throughout the entire first twelve months—rhyming books, books with repetition, touch and feel books, and books with sounds that your child can imitate. Each type of literature has its own benefits; besides, the baby enjoys seeing and hearing familiar sights and sounds.

The following chart gives the characteristics of infant development adapted from *The First Three Years of Life* by Burton White, with ways to relate the sharing of literature to each characteristic and suggestions for particularly appropriate books.[6]

LITERATURE FOR INFANTS

Characteristics	*Activities*	*Suggested Books**
Birth to Around Six Months		
Exploring by listening: receiving language.	Read books that "sound good"—that *you* enjoy reading; sing songs.	Mother Goose, adult poetry, the *Bible*, repetitive stories, lullabies, songs, adult books.
Exploring by feeling: reaching out.	Read books that provide different textures; help child to turn pages.	"Touch Books" like *Pat the Bunny* *The Touch Me Book* *The Very Hungry Caterpillar*
Exploring by gumming.	Let infant have teething ring or toy while you are reading; read aloud while feeding.	

LITERATURE FOR INFANTS

Characteristics	*Activities*	*Suggested Books**
Exploring by looking.	Try books with large, clear pictures, especially those with faces.	*What Animals Do* *The Teddy-Board Series* *Brimax Books*

Six Months to About One Year

Small object play.	Let child hold a small object while you read; participation books.	*The Very Hungry Caterpillar* *Pat the Bunny*
Developing memory and "object permanence" (the concept that something does not go away even when covered).	Pick an object illustrated in the book and let child find the page it is on; repeat stories; look at photograph albums of family members.	ABC books like *Gyo Fujikawa's* *A to Z Picture Book* *What Animals Do* *Inch by Inch*
Developing curiosity.	Read stories that start on one page and end on the next page; books that ask questions.	*Ask Mr. Bear* *Goodnight Owl* *Surprise, Surprise* *Do You Want To Be My Friend?*

LITERATURE FOR INFANTS

Characteristics	Activities	Suggested Books*
Learning names for things.	Point as you name things.	*Early Words* ABC books *The Teddy-Board Series*
Developing recognition of mother and father.	Books with mommy and daddy in them; photograph albums.	*Pat the Bunny* *Little Gorilla* *The Carrot Seed*
Continuing language development: sounds.	Songs, lullabies, rhymes, repetition.	*Mother Goose* *Goodnight Moon*
Continuing language development: sentences.	Repetitious books.	*Goodnight Owl* *Ask Mr. Bear* *Rosie's Walk* *Animals of Farmer Jones*

*See the booklist, p. 12, for authors' names and other details about the suggested books.

How Do I Read with My Infant?

Guidelines that can be followed for successful reading sessions with an infant include:

1. Read when you are in a positive mood, when you feel like relaxing and would enjoy the experience.
2. Select something *you* would like to read.
3. Read when the infant is likely to want to sit still for

a story. Just after a nap or before bed seem to be good times, for the child is just winding up or winding down from a more active period. The best times for reading, however, are different for each child. Have regular times for reading, and read at special times as well.

4. Settle the child down for reading, perhaps by turning on the light and saying, "light."

5. Be sure that an infant old enough to look at pictures can see the book you are reading. You can read while feeding a newborn, or while rocking with him in a chair. You can make a simple book rack from a 12" × 18" piece of ¼" plywood by screwing hooks into it to support your book while you hold the newborn with two hands. But for the infant who is old enough to hold his head up and focus on a picture, lap reading is the most fun.

6. Make reading a comfortable experience. Be sure your baby is warm enough, but not too warm. Sitting on your lap, she will be warmer than when playing independently. Be sure you are comfortable. Some families have a chair for story reading with a lamp to light the book. The child gets used to hearing a story when sitting in that special chair.

7. Be responsive. Parent educators call it *synchrony* —you and the child are on the same wavelength. If the child reaches out, encourage the reaching and linger on that page for a longer time. But if the child is starting to get restless, speed up the story, change the words, skip a page. At this age the child is not going to know the difference. And if she fusses or looks away, put away the book and go back to reading at another time.

8. Let the child help turn the pages. Keep all the unread pages except the next one to be turned in your right hand, so that the child will turn only one page at a time.

9. Point to things in pictures as you are reading. When your infant starts reaching out, he will naturally point

too. You can then encourage pointing by telling the child what is being pointed out.

10. Go over the book a second time—not reading it all but just stopping at favorite pictures.

11. Use your voice effectively. Basically a soft, quiet voice that will calm your infant and sound pleasing is best. Occasionally be expressive and dramatic. Change your voice for different characters. Use sound effects that will encourage your child's participation, but that won't provoke fear. (Remember, you don't need to shout—your infant's ear is close to your mouth.) Read as though you are having fun—ideally you will be.

12. When your child is teething and takes everything into his mouth, you might try giving him something quiet to chew on while you are reading, like a finger (not keys). When the child is grabbing (and tearing paper), give him something soft—a stuffed animal, perhaps—to hold while you read aloud. He will be more likely to pull at the animal than at the book.

13. In your story reading, repeat a few familiar books over and over; at the same time, introduce new stories. Read several books at one sitting if the infant is enjoying the reading. Start with something old, read something new, and then finish with a familiar selection.

14. End gently. Talk about the book and then gradually move on to a new activity. Store the books on a shelf where the child can see them, and not with the child's toys. Books are not toys and should not be treated as such.

There are several things you should *not* do:

1. Don't read when *you* don't feel like it.
2. Don't read a story you don't enjoy.
3. Don't let the child tear the pages of books. Keep

easily damaged books out of your infant's reach when there is no supervision.

4. Don't put books in the playpen where they are likely to be kicked, torn, and chewed.

Your Home Reading Environment

It is never too soon to begin a collection of books for a child. They make excellent baby gifts. Store your infant's books at adult eye level so the baby can see then when he is being held. Shelve books with colorful covers face out so that your infant can see them and learn to recognize the book corner. When she begins to crawl, a low shelf for sturdy cardboard books will encourage the child to seek out books independently.

Babies can be taught to handle books properly. According to Annis Duff, children will not love and respect books if their own books don't interest them or if they are allowed to abuse them.[7] Some parent education books advocate letting babies tear old newspapers and magazines, but we believe these should only be torn when they are to be used in art projects. Magazines and newspapers are forms of literature which a baby (and later toddler) will enjoy along with books.

You might try to have at least one time during the day when a place in your home is quiet, calm, and well lit for reading. Noise and motion will attract an infant—and distract him from listening to you read.

How Can We Develop Good Family Reading Habits?

With books readily available, you can establish a routine for reading with your infant several times during the day.

You might read regularly during feedings, or have a set time to read to and rock your child. Your infant will begin to associate reading with the regular daily schedule. Phyllis Fenner, a children's book specialist and author, quotes Mary Ellen Coe, a parent who recalls that "Mother read during her 'respite' at 11 in the red rocking chair by the window."[8]

Families enjoy reading together at holiday times and on trips. While you are driving on errands around town, try singing to your infant and chanting nursery rhymes or telling stories. On longer jaunts, the adult who is not driving can read to the rest of the family—infant included.

You might make a tape of yourself chanting rhymes or reading a favorite story, and play it while you are busy working around the house. When you are away from home, babysitters might play the tape to the child.

How Can We Develop Good Family Library Habits?

Even infants enjoy a change of scene once in a while and the library is a pleasant, calm place to visit. Many libraries have toys for infants to play with while their parents are selecting books. If your library does not have such a service, perhaps you could organize a neighborhood group to collect used but durable and unbroken toys that could be donated to your local library for this purpose. Some libraries have a special section of cardboard books, and books with bright pictures for the very young.

The wall decorations of the children's room at the library are attractive for infants. If, for example, nursery rhymes are pictured on the wall, you might recite the rhymes while your infant looks at the characters. One library has a peep show where tiny children can peer through little holes at a well-lighted dollhouse with favorite storybook characters in it. Books with colorful jackets are often on display. Libraries that offer no services for infants might respond to suggestions from parents that they do so.

How Can I Involve My Infant with Literature in Other Ways?

You can *tell* stories to your infant—just the sound of your voice is appealing. Make up stories; they need not be elaborate, factual, or detailed. Tell your infant about your day, your youth, your hopes. Tell a fairy tale. Just talking with your infant as you feed, carry, clothe, or change diapers, gives her a sense of language and a sense of story.

Sing to your infant—popular songs and hymns that you enjoy as well as children's songs and lullabies. Finger plays and songs or chants with motions will captivate the older infant. Remember "Pat-a-cake," "Pease Porridge Hot," and "Pony Boy?"

Selected Booklist

There are three essentials that will serve as the core of a collection of books for every infant: Mother Goose; a children's song book; and the classic *Arbuthnot Anthology of Children's Literature* (new fourth edition, published by Lothrop, Lee and Shepard). Each will give you a variety of rhymes, poems, songs, and stories to enjoy with your baby. Each will last well beyond the infant years.

Beyond these basic three you can begin collecting at least four different types of books: books of rhymes and songs; "point and say" books; books to touch; and stories for very young children. Recommending specific titles can be risky since most parents have their own favorites. The following list gives some suggestions for literature for infants as well as ideas for involving your infant with books. How you read with your infant is just as important as the fact that you are doing it.

Musical Literature and Nursery Rhymes

The literature infants enjoy earliest is the musical literature of lullabies, songs, and nursery rhymes. You can sing, chant, or read aloud as you rock your newborn child. Many nursery rhymes and songs fit into daily routines. Sing "Good morning to you" as the infant awakens; try "Hickory Dickory Dock" in front of the clock; sing "Rub-a-dub-dub" and "Row, Row, Row Your Boat" as tub songs; "Diddle, diddle dumpling" can accompany getting dressed. Look at an extensive Mother Goose collection and you will see that the possibilities for this sort of natural chanting and singing are endless. Although at first singing and chanting is not *reading* with the child, it won't be long before your baby can hear these by now familiar rhymes and songs as you share a book. What fun you will have when you see that your baby actually recognizes the verses!

There are many nursery rhyme collections and books of songs. Find ones that are quite comprehensive. Some include music and directions for finger plays. In addition, find some shorter collections or individual song books for the baby. It will help to have some easy-to-

carry rhyme books for trips and some for your home,
some sturdy ones for baby to look at and touch and some
paperbacks for light traveling. An index is helpful when
you want to locate a special rhyme quickly. You might
choose from among the following collections:

Glazer, Tom. *Eye Winker, Tom Tinker, Chin Chopper: A
    Collection of Musical Finger Plays*. Garden City,
    N.Y.: Doubleday, 1973.
    This paperback collection of fifty musical finger
    plays includes directions for finger motions and
    musical scores for each song.
Opie, Iona and Peter. *The Oxford Dictionary of Nursery
    Rhymes*. London: Oxford University Press, 1951.
    This exhaustive reference is for the parent who is
    interested in learning about histories of rhymes and
    word definitions as well as singing nursery rhymes.
    The book contains more than 800 well-known and
    rare rhymes and songs. It is probably the definitive
    collection of nursery rhymes.
Porter, Elizabeth. *Baby's Song Book*. New York: Thomas
    Y. Crowell, 1972.
    Music is provided in this edition of songs for little
    ones.
Rossetti, Christina G. *Sing Song: A Nursery Rhyme
    Book*. Illus: Arthur Hughes. New York: Dover, 1969.
    Musical nursery rhymes (including the music) are
    found in this edition.

Collections that your infant will enjoy when he is old
enough to look at pictures include:

Battaglia, Aurelius. *Mother Goose*. New York: Random
    House, 1973.
    This small paperback is easy to carry.

Chorao, Kay. *The Baby's Lap Book.* New York: E. P. Dutton, 1977.

The Mother Goose rhymes are illustrated in grey sketches with one verse on each page. The drawings are beautiful and provide a contrast to the color which most baby books contain.

Fujikawa, Gyo. *Mother Goose.* New York: Grosset and Dunlap, 1975.

This large format book comes in both hardback and paperback editions. Several rhymes appear on each page, each with its own illustration.

Petersham, Maud and Miska. *The Rooster Crows.* New York: Macmillan, 1945.

Broader than Mother Goose, this collection includes traditional American songs and has large realistic illustrations.

Potter, Beatrix. *Appley Dapply's Nursery Rhymes; Cecily Parsley's Nursery Rhymes.* New York: Frederick Warne.

These tiny books with parts of a verse on each page are great fun to read with your infant. Pages are sturdy enough for the baby to turn.

Rojankovsky, Feodor. *The Tall Book of Mother Goose.* New York: Harper & Row, 1942.

The tall, thin size makes this volume unique. One rhyme appears on each page.

Tudor, Tasha. *Mother Goose.* New York: Henry Z. Walck, 1976.

The small size and realistic illustrations make this a suitable edition for infants.

Wilkins, Eloise. *Ladybug, Ladybug.* New York: Random House, 1979.

This small cardboard, spiral-bound nursery rhyme book contains common verses, one on a page with a matching picture.

Wright, Blanche F. *The Real Mother Goose*. Chicago,
Illinois: Rand McNally, 1978.

This large, popular edition does not have realistic
pictures, nor is there a picture to match each rhyme,
but the illustrations are big and bright.

Point and Say Books

As your infant gets older (2–4 months) and begins focusing on pictures, you can seek out books with colorful,
clear, realistic, and uncluttered illustrations, especially
books that match your baby's own experience—books
about familiar kinds of people, pets and other animals,
toys, food, cars, and trucks. In this category books illustrated with photographs are especially good.

When "reading" this type of literature, point to each
item in the picture while naming it clearly, then talk
about it. "See the high chair? That looks like Laurel's
high chair." After much adult pointing and naming, your
infant will learn to point to the picture when you ask,
"Where's the puppy dog? Can you point to the puppy
dog?"

There are several series of "point and say" books.

Bruna, Dick (many titles). New York: Methuen. A partial
list of titles includes: *Another Story to Tell; I Can
Count; I Can Count More; I Can Dress Myself; I
Can Read Difficult Words; I Can Read More; The
King; Miffy; Miffy at the Beach; Miffy in the Hospi-
tal; Snuffy*.

These small books have very simple, clear, uncluttered pictures in bright primary colors, including
some drawings of faces, and an equally simple text.

First Step Series: Bedtime; Mealtime; Playtime; etc.
London: Brimax Books, 1973.

An English series, available in bookstores and libraries in this country, these hard-paged books show routine things that are fun to talk about with the baby.

The Lady Bird Series: *The Ladybird ABC*. London: (Loughborough: The Ladybird Books, Ltd.) 1961.

Readily available in bookstores in this country, this series has clear pictures of common objects. The books are small and easy for an infant to manipulate. *The Ladybird ABC* is a good one to start with, since it has only one object on each page.

Teddy-Board Books: Baby's First Book; Baby's First Toys; Baby Animals; etc. New York: Platt and Munk.

Several of these books are excellent first books for infants. They are spiral-bound cardboard books that open flat. The pictures are of common things, very clearly illustrated in color.

Wolde, Gunilla. *Betsy Books*. New York: Random House.

There are several books in this series of stories about Betsy. Some titles include *Betsy's Baby Brother; Betsy and Peter are Different;* and *Betsy and the Vacuum Cleaner*.

ABC and counting books, as well as word books, are good for "point and say" reading.

Broomfield, Robert. *The Baby Animal ABC*. New York: Penguin, 1968.

This paperback has very realistic pictures of several animal babies for each letter of the alphabet.

Cellini. *ABC*. New York: Grosset and Dunlap, 1975.

A tall, hard-paged book with very clear pictures that an infant can easily identify.

Curry, Nancy. *An Apple Is Red*. Los Angeles: Bowmar, 1977.
  Colorful, clear photographs illustrate this little volume.
Dunn, P. and T. *Things*. Garden City, N.Y.: Doubleday, 1968.
  Infants will be able to study the clear, color photographs that illustrate this book.
Fujikawa, Gyo. *Gyo Fujikawa's A to Z Picture Book*. New York: Grosset and Dunlap, 1974.
  A large-format volume with many pictures of people, animals, and objects, some in color and some in black and white. This book has numerous talking possibilities. Develop little routines for each page: sing "Pop goes the Weasel" when you point to the weasel; jump baby on your lap for the jump page, etc.
Matthiesen, Thomas. *ABC: An Alphabet Book*. New York: Platt and Munk, 1968.
  Again, beautiful and clear illustrations make this book a natural for infants.
Pfloog, Jan. *Animals on the Farm*. New York: Golden Press, 1977.
  Infants can learn animal sounds as they identify the realistic animal pictures.
Rojankovsky, Feodor. *Animals in the Zoo*. New York: Alfred A. Knopf, 1962.
  Animals are a favorite subject for infants. This large-sized book contains lovely, realistic illustrations.
Scarry, Richard. *Early Words*. New York: Random House, 1976.
  The rabbits in this book have common objects in their homes, such as sinks, toothbrushes, tables, and chairs, that your baby can recognize. It is an ideal book for pointing and naming.

Weisgard, Leonard. *My First Picture Book*. New York: Grosset and Dunlap, 1964.
Realistic drawings of common items make this a good "point and say" book.

Touching and Smelling Books

Infants use all of their senses to explore their environment. A number of books have capitalized on babies' desires to touch and smell things. Textured pages invite infants to touch and pull them. Most of the books listed below are more toys than books, but they will provide an initial involvement with books for your infant.

The Look, Look Book; Pat the Bunny; The Telephone Book; The Touch Me Book; What's in Mommy's Pocketbook?; Who Lives Here?; and others. New York: Golden Press.
Each book of these touch books is small and has especially strong cardboard pages. First, show the baby what to do on each page, then have him try it himself. You could make books like *The Touch Me Book* out of materials in your home—sandpaper, an emory board, velvet, corduroy, or silk.
Golden Scratch and Sniff Books.
In this series, if you scratch the item in the picture, you release an odor. These are probably too complex for all but the oldest infants.
Sniffy Books; Lowly Worm Sniffy Book; Papa's Pizza; The Sniff and Tell Riddle Book; Supermarket Magic, and others. New York: Random House.
Similar to the Golden Books above, these are probably more appropriate for toddlers than infants, because infants may not have a sophisticated enough sense of smell to identify odors like that of pizza.

Carle, Eric. *The Very Hungry Caterpillar*. Cleveland:
Collins-World, 1969.
Not published specifically for infants, and very
popular with older children, this story of a caterpillar becoming a butterfly by eating holes through the
pages of the book (each of which represents a food)
will delight the infant who is reaching out. Your
child's tiny fingers will fit through the holes and the
pages of various sizes will be very easy for baby to
turn.

Cardboard Books

As your infant begins to reach out, he needs sturdy books
that he can look at independently. Tall, thin, sturdy
books are fun to take for reading on car rides, since the
narrow pages are easy to turn.

Look at Us. London: Brimax Books, 1975.
The illustrations in this hard-paged book are photo-
graphs clear enough for very young infants to recog-
nize.
Fujikawa, Gyo. *Our Best Friends; Sleepytime; Surprise,
Surprise*; and many others. New York: Grosset and
Dunlap.
Some of Fujikawa's hard-paged books are more ap-
propriate for toddlers, but these three have very
clear pictures. *Surprise, Surprise* is fun just before
bath time or water play.
Golden Sturdy Books: *I Am A Bunny; I Am A Puppy;
I Am A Kitten; I Am A Mouse*. New York: Golden
Press.
Point to things as you name them or read the simple
stories. *I Am A Kitten* and *I Am A Puppy* are espe-

cially good after baby has been to a pet store and
seen a kitten or puppy. *I Am A Bunny* is a real favorite because of all the other animals in it.

McNaught, Harry. *Baby Animals*. New York: Random
House, 1976.
McNaught's animals are very clearly drawn. You can
make animal sounds as well as name them.

Miller, J. P. *Farmer John's Animals*. New York: Random
House, 1979.
You can follow Farmer John around the farm as he
does his chores and make the animal sounds as the
animals ask for supper in this spiral-bound
cardboard book.

Pfloog, Jan. *Kittens*. New York: Random House, 1977.
When pointing out cats in this book you can make all
sorts of comparisons.

———. *Puppies*. New York: Random House, 1979.
A companion volume to *Kittens*, the illustrations are
charming in this cardboard book.

Scarry, Richard. *What Animals Do*. New York: Golden
Press, 1968.
A tall, thin book with one simple sentence on each
page such as, "The Kangaroo hops." Baby has fun
turning the pages of this as you read. After reading
once, go back and read it again, but change the
words into questions. For example, "Does the kangaroo run?" "No—the kangaroo hops."

———. *Is This the House of Mistress Mouse?* New York:
Golden Press, 1964.
One hole through each page leading to a fuzzy ball
at the end encourages touching. Your infant will also
enjoy following the mouse through the story.

Schlesinger, Alice. *Baby's Mother Goose*. New York:
Grosset and Dunlap, 1975.
Point to each rhyme as you say or sing it. Soon baby

will point to ask for the rhyme herself. See if baby
can find a favorite rhyme. Later, when baby is about
a year old, let her complete rhymes and use the book
for independent reading.

Wells, Rosemary. *Max's First Word Book* ("delicious"
is the first word); *Max's New Suit* (in which Max)
dresses himself); *Max's Ride* (concepts of over, under, etc.); and *Max's Toys* (counting). New York:
Dial Press, 1979.
These small cardboard books are a bit didactic, but
involve everyday situations which infants can recognize.

Farm Animals. New York: Grosset and Dunlap, 1974.
This is another tall cardboard book good for pointing
to the animals and naming them.

Cloth Books and Plastic Books

Cloth books and plastic books that squeak and make
other noises are more properly classified as toys. Infants
have difficulty handling cloth books. Also, if they become accustomed to cloth books, they may be tempted to
treat paper books as roughly as the cloth. Generally cloth
books are not as useful for infants as sturdier books. If
they are used at all, they are best left in the playpen or
crib for baby to play with as a toy. Several publishers
have cloth book series available. Only one book (*My Zoo
Book*, published by Platt and Munk) is illustrated with
realistic photographs.

Cindell, Eva. *My Bedtime Book*. Illus: George DeSantis.
New York: Platt and Munk. This is one of a series of
Platt and Munk cloth books called "Perma-Life
Books."

Dean's Washable Cloth Books. Dean's Rag Book
Company.

DeMuth, Vivienne. *The Busy Animal Dress-up Book.*
New York: Gingerbread House, 1979.

Ford, George. *Baby's First Picture Book.* New York:
Random House, 1979.

Johnson, Evelyne. *Fun in the Tub.* Illus: Tien. New
York: Gingerbread House, 1979.

Johnson, John E. *The Me Book.* New York: Random
House, 1979.

Puppet Cloth Books: *Baby's Farm Animals; Baby's
Mother Goose; See What Baby Can Do.* New York:
Grosset and Dunlap.

Rand McNally. Cloth Books.

Scarry, Richard. *Huckle's Book.* New York: Random
House, 1979.

Smollin, Mike. *The Cow Says Moo.* New York: Random
House, 1979.

————. *Your Friends from Sesame Street.* Random
House, 1979.

Winship, Florence Sarah. *Mother Goose.* New York:
Golden Press, 1959. This is one of a series called
"Baby's First Golden Cloth Books."

Early Stories

As your infant becomes able to sit up in your lap and look
at pictures, you can begin to read simple stories. They
should have few words per page and contain repetitious
word patterns. Be sure there is a central character who
appears on each page.

Bornstein, Ruth. *Little Gorilla.* New York: Seabury,
1976.

As little gorilla grows up, he appears a little bit
larger on each page.

Brown, Margaret Wise. *Goodnight Moon*. New York:
Harper & Row, 1947.

This classic has survived (and is now available in
paperback) because it is a perfect book for babies. It
is a grand book for pointing. First you point at things
while naming them; then baby will point and you
name them. Later ask the baby, "Where is the
mouse?" and she will point it out. The story is in
rhyme. If *Goodnight Moon* is read before bedtime
when the moon is out, your infant is likely to become quite excited about it.

————. *The Golden Egg Book*. Illus: Leonard Weisgard,
Golden Press, 1976.

Another classic that has been reissued (1946), this
large-sized book invites your infant to guess what is
in the egg.

Carle, Eric. *Do You Want to Be My Friend?* New York:
Thomas Y. Crowell, 1971.

This picture book has one large illustration of an
animal (kangaroo, lion, etc.) on each page and a little
mouse who goes along obviously asking each animal
to be his friend (though there is no text accompanying the pictures). Before turning each page, you see
the tail of the animal that is about to be pictured.
Toddlers can try guessing which animal will appear
from this "hint." Infants can learn to name the animals and find the mouse.

Flack, Marjorie. *Angus and the Cat*. Garden City, N.Y.:
Doubleday, 1931.

Another long-time favorite now in paperback, this
one has a simple story, animal sounds, and a cat to
follow on each page. There are several other Angus
books for older children.

————. *Ask Mr. Bear*. New York: Macmillan, 1958. Paperback edition, 1971.

In our opinion, this book is one that should not be missed by any child of about 10 months to one year old. It is very repetitious and has clear pictures of animals. The child will learn animal sounds from it. (The bear hug at the end is an extra dividend for you, the parent.)

Gale, Leah. *The Animals of Farmer Jones*. Illus.: Richard Scarry. New York: Golden Press, 1970.

There are excellent, clear pictures of each farm animal asking for its supper and, in turn, receiving it. The story line includes animal sounds.

Hutchins, Pat. *Good Night Owl*. New York: Macmillan, 1968.

A very repetitive book (. . . "and owl tried to sleep"). Point to each bird or animal as you read each page. Soon baby will point as you read and will begin to make the animal sounds. "Owl," "bee," and "moon" will become early words. Go outside to see the moon if you read this at night. Visit a museum or zoo to see an owl.

————. *Rosie's Walk*. New York: Macmillan, 1968.

Rosie the hen goes for a walk and is oblivious to the fox who is following her. Older infants may get the humor; younger ones will enjoy following Rosie and the fox on each page.

Krauss, Ruth. *The Carrot Seed*. Illus: Crockett Johnson. New York: Harper & Row, 1945. Paperback edition, 1976.

A boy plants a carrot which finally grows. If your infant is around when you are planting a garden, this would be a good, simple book to share.

Lionni, Leo. *Inch by Inch*. New York: Astor-Honor, 1962.

The inchworm appears on each page. Baby will enjoy turning the pages and finding it as you read the story.

Nakatani, Chiyoko. *My Teddy Bear*. New York: Thomas Y. Crowell, 1976.

A little book about a teddy bear that will appeal to the infant who has a teddy bear of her own.

Petersham, Maud and Miska. *The Box with Red Wheels*. New York: Macmillan, 1949. Paperback edition, 1973.

Lots of animals visit an infant in this story, and the box with red wheels appears on each page.

Polushkin, Maria. *Who Said Meow?* Illus: G. Maestro. New York: Crown, 1975.

Puppy searches all over to find the source of the "meow." See if your infant can find the cat on each page as you read the "meow" sound. Later, baby will learn to say "meow" in the right places himself.

Notes

[1] May L. Becker, *First Adventures in Reading: Introducing Children to Books* (New York: F. A. Stokes, 1936) p. 2.

[2] Annis Duff, *"Bequest of Wings" A Family's Pleasure with Books* (New York: Viking, 1944), p. 17.

[3] Nancy Larrick, "Home Influences on Early Readings." *Today's Education, 64* (November–December, 1975) 77–79.

[4] Becker, p. 2

[5] Ibid., p. 6

[6] Burton L. White, *The First Three Years of LIFE* (Englewood Cliffs, N.J.: Prentice-Hall, 1975)

[7] Duff, p. 17.

[8] Phyllis Fenner, *Something Shared: Children and Books* (New York: John Day, 1959)

References

Arbuthnot, May Hill. *Children's Reading in the Home*. New York: Lothrop, Lee and Shepard, 1969.

Becker, May L. *First Adventures in Reading: Introducing Children to Books*. New York: F. A. Stokes, 1936.

Berg, Lela. *Reading and Loving*. London: Heineman, 1976.

Duff, Annis. *"Bequest of Wings" A Family's Pleasure with Books*. New York: Viking, 1944.

Farjeon, Eleanor. *The Little Bookworm*. New York: Henry Z. Walck, 1956.

Fenner, Phyllis. *Something Shared: Children and Books*. New York: John Day, 1959.

Frank, Josette. *Your Child's Reading Today*. Garden City, N.Y. Doubleday, 1969.

Gordon, Ira J. *The Infant Experience*. Columbus, Ohio: Charles E. Merrill, 1975.

Johnson, Ferne. *Start Early for an Early Start: You and the Young Child*. Chicago: American Library Association, 1976.

Lanes, Selma. *Down the Rabbit Hole*. New York: Atheneum, 1977.

Larrick, Nancy. "Home Influences on Early Reading." *Today's Education, 64* (November–December, 1975).

McCann, Donnarae. *The Child's First Books*. Bronx, N.Y.: H. W. Wilson, 1973.

White, Burton L. *The First Three Years of LIFE*. Englewood Cliffs, N.J.: Prentice-Hall, 1975.

II

Sharing Literature with Your Toddler

Ages 1 to 3

There is little need to justify sharing literature with toddlers, but for those seeking reasons, a researcher named Irwin found that parents' systematic story reading to toddlers from 13 to 30 months old was an aid in their language development.[1]

Of course sharing literature with your toddler yields lots of other benefits. It encourages close physical encounters between parent and child that are pleasant for both; it helps develop reading readiness skills; and it teaches toddlers to enjoy and value books. The child becomes familiar with print and illustrations, learns about story characters and plots, learns the sounds that letters stand for, and begins to rhyme words. These and other prereading skills will come naturally. The skills aren't "taught" as much as they are "caught."

Annis Duff considered books as "pleasant necessities:"

"People often said to us, "How does it happen that your children know so many books? Mine have never asked for them." It does not just happen; children seldom do *ask* for books, as an initial stage in learning to love them. Reading, for young children, is rarely a pleasure in isolation, but comes through shared pleasure and constant discerning exposure to books so that they fall naturally into the category of pleasant necessities, along with food, sleep, music and all out-of-doors."[2]

Somewhere between the ages of 12 and 18 months, your baby will begin to walk. Walking signals a change in your child's reaction to being read to. Instead of sitting passively on your lap while you sing or read, your toddler will want to select books, to participate, to move around, and to have some books read over and over and over again! You will need new approaches to share literature effectively and enjoyably with your active child.

What is Good Literature for a Toddler?

The kinds of books you choose to share with your toddler will depend to some extent upon her previous encounters with books. The toddler who has been read to since birth knows by now not to tear pages and to handle books gently.

Toddlers need variety in the literature they encounter. In addition to newspapers, magazines, food containers, mail, and other everyday printed materials, they like all sorts of books: big books, little books, collections, individual stories, poetry, prose, songs, cardboard books, and paperbacks. For lap reading, books "two laps wide," as May Becker described them, like *London Bridge* or *Millions of Cats*, are good. For carrying around the house, car trips, or just variety, little books like *Peter Rabbit* and *The Nutshell Library* are fun. Thick collections, such as *My Book House, Childcraft*, or Mother Goose collections, encourage longer read-aloud sessions, while books containing only one rhyme (*Three Jovial Huntsmen*) are better when time is limited.

Phyllis Fenner says "We concern ourselves much too seriously with *what* a child reads. *That* he reads should be our first concern."[3] For a toddler, this is especially true. Your toddler may become just as attached to a fifty-nine cent drugstore book as to an expensive, beautifully illustrated picture book. In Annis Duff's home, even very tiny children had definite book preferences.[4]

In general, books with clear, bright illustrations and a simple text with only a few words to a page will have immediate appeal. However, picturebooks that use abstract art forms or are in muted colors should also be read. Since books are a child's first encounter with artwork, we need to provide exposure to abstract as well as realistic illustration. Books should give the child opportunities for involvement—for singing, pretending to read, acting out, touching—and if you see that your toddler takes advantage of these opportunities, he will become an eager, active "reader."

Books with repetition also have great appeal. Your toddler can understand what is being read better than an infant can. Thus, reading can provide new experiences, prepare her for new events, develop values, impart useful information, and provide entertainment.[5]

What are the characteristics of a toddler and how can we help toddlers enjoy literature once we understand them? The following chart will help answer these questions. The characteristics of typical child development are adapted from Burton White's classic, *The First Three Years of Life.*[6]

LITERATURE FOR TODDLERS

Characteristic	*Activities*	*Suggested Books**
Learning to talk: one word; new words.	Books with key words, common words; books to point at, name things, talk about.	*A Peaceable Kingdom* *Gyo Fujikawa's A to Z Book* *Anybody at Home?* *ABC of Cars and Trucks* *Clocks and More Clocks* *Kittens are Like That* *Baby Animals* *We Went Looking* *Once We Went on a Picnic*
Learning to talk: simple sentences.	Books with very short, simple sentences and repetition.	*Goodnight Owl* *The Happy Day* *What Animals Do* *Ask Mr. Bear* *Too Much Noise*
Crawling, climbing and running.	Books stored in many places; stories that child can act out.	*The Gunniwolf* *Just Me* *The Gingerbread Man* *Caps for Sale*

LITERATURE FOR TODDLERS

Characteristics	*Activities*	*Suggested Books**
Pride in personal accomplishment; growing independence.	Pages for child to turn; very simple stories that child can learn to "read" independently through hearing them often.	*The Happy Egg* Alphabet books with one word per page *The Happy Day*
Developing a sense of humor; curiosity; guessing.	Funny stories; stories with suspense that require turning one or more pages to learn how they end.	*Rosie's Walk* *A Woggle of Witches* *Oh A-Hunting We Will Go* *Who Said Meow?* *Angus and the Cat* *Three Little Pigs* *Nutshell Library* *It does Not Say Meow*
Social development; character development.	Endearing character that can be followed through a story.	*Swimmy* *Corduroy* *Inch by Inch* *Tale of Peter Rabbit* *Thy Friend, Obadiah* *Beady Bear* *Mike Mulligan*
Exploring objects; manipulating things.	Small books the child can play with; books about	*Feed the Animals* *See the Circus* *Changes, Changes* *The Grouchy Ladybug*

LITERATURE FOR TODDLERS

Characteristics	Activities	Suggested Books*
	things a child can play with.	*Nutshell Library* *Most Amazing Hide-and-Seek Alphabet Book*
Interest in change.	Books that include changes (day/night; things growing).	*The Very Hungry Caterpillar* *My Day on the Farm* *Goodnight Moon* *The Maggie B* *The Carrot Seed* *Mushroom in the Rain*
Interest in primary caretakers.	Stories about mothers and fathers.	*Runaway Bunny* *Ask Mr. Bear* *The Three Bears* *Over the River and Through the woods* *Little Gorilla* *Where Did My Mother Go?* *Whose Mouse Are You?* *Whistle for Willie* *Little Hippo*
Developing positive sibling relationships.	Stories about siblings.	*Rachel and Obadiah* *The Maggie B*
Testing adults; testing limits; negativism.	Books that ask questions the child can answer with, "No!".	*Ask Mr. Bear* *Caps for Sale* *Who Said Meow?*

LITERATURE FOR TODDLERS

Characteristics	*Activities*	*Suggested Books**
Playing make believe; pretending.	Make-believe stories.	*Just Me* *Runaway Bunny* *A Rainbow of My Own*
Learning colors.	Stories with pictures in clear colors.	*A Panda Is Black and White* *Lisa and Lynn* *Caps for Sale* *My Very First Book of Colors*
Learning to Count.	Books with counting; books with clear numbers in them.	*My Big Golden Counting Book* *Over in the Meadow* *Seven Little Rabbits* *One is Johnny* *Never Tease a Weasel*
Learning to rhyme words.	Rhyming stories and songs.	*In a Pumpkin Shell* *Over in the Meadow* *Oh A-Hunting We Will Go* *Chicken Soup with Rice* *Where Does a Butterfly Go When It Rains?* *The Erie Canal* *Hot Cross Buns* *London Bridge is Falling Down* *Yankee Doodle* *Hush, Little Baby* *Mother Goose*

*See the booklist, p. 41, for authors' names and other details about the suggested books.

How Do I Read with My Toddler?

There are two keys to having a successful reading experience with a toddler. One is to have a regular routine and the other, to provide variety. Toddlers like to hear the same story or poem or song over and over. They delight in the routine of reading at the same time and in the same place every day. But they also like surprises— different books read in new and different places.

James Flood, a professor at Boston University, in a study of 36 parents reading *Ask Mr. Bear* to their children, found these important components of a parent-child reading session: You should involve children verbally in the story and let them interact with you while you are reading. In good story-reading sessions the children talked a lot, asking and answering questions. Parents asked warm-up questions before reading and evaluative questions after reading and gave positive reinforcement to their children while reading to them.[7]

In addition, the following guidelines may be helpful.

1. Establish a routine time and place for reading aloud. Make sure you are in a quiet place where you will not be disturbed. Your child will grow to value reading with you when he sees that your time together is so important that it is rarely interrupted.

2. Have your reading session when your toddler is likely to sit still—early in the morning, just before or after nap time, or just before bedtime.

3. Select books yourself and have the toddler select others so that you can read several books at one sitting and have alternatives at hand if the child balks at a particular title.

4. Settle in. You and the child should both be comfortable. Some children prefer to sit on their parent's lap; others do not.

5. Read a familiar story first, with the child participating. Then go to something new, and finish with another familiar book.

6. Let the child put the books back and select another if she wants to hear more.

7. Involve the toddler with reading: Have him turn pages of familiar stories, or leave out the last word of a rhyme and have the child supply it. Have the child point to or identify things as you read about them. Ask him to guess what will happen next (if the story allows). Or make a game of your questions—"Is it a pie? Is it a cake? Is it a cookie? Oh, it's a pudding!"

8. Choose other than routine times and places to read—in your bed, on the floor (the toddler can sit between your crossed legs), at the table while waiting for a meal, in the bathtub, while you are working in the kitchen (baby can turn pages while you glance down at a familiar story), in the car, or anywhere outdoors.

9. Encourage your toddler to look at books independently by providing a little moveable stool or chair, and putting books in a variety of places around the house.

10. After you have read a story, encourage the child to go back and look at the pictures.

11. Point things out in the pictures as you are reading and encourage your toddler to do likewise.

12. Read in a soft voice, but with expression.

13. Stop reading the minute your child wants to stop.

14. Finally, the most important message is: Read to your child *frequently!*

Your Home Reading Environment

You should consider the reading environment as a part of the child's total home experience. Toddlers need to see and do new things. One parent found that her 2½-year-old related her reading directly to her own life. She says, "Over and over again I see that her reading enjoyment is contingent upon the range of her previous experience."[8]

Toddlers enjoy carrying books around with them. Try having several places to store books: a cardboard box near a toy shelf, a low bookshelf near where parents' books are shelved, in the crib for reading before and after nap time, in the car, and in a box in the kitchen. Toddlers like to be near adults, so it helps to place books where you spend a lot of time. Keep more valuable books, like anthologies, on a high shelf out of the child's reach for when you read with him.

Think of reading material for your home in broader terms than just as books. Let your toddler "read" newspapers, magazines, food containers, and personal letters, and teach her to treat all printed material with the same respect and care she gives to books.

Make sure that your home includes some cozy spots for reading, away from television and other distractions. A big soft pillow in a corner, a rocking chair, a comfortable stuffed chair—with good lighting—will encourage every member of your family to read. Read with your toddler in a variety of places and read a variety of things. He will enjoy hearing adults and older children read aloud to each other as well as hearing his own special stories read to him.

How Can We Develop Good Family Reading Habits?

If you have begun collecting books for your toddler and have been reading to her since she was an infant, she is already developing good reading habits. There are scheduled times for reading together and for reading independently. Routine times and places for reading help establish the reading habit.

You continue to sing and chant rhymes as you go about your daily activities, only now your toddler makes requests and joins in. Keep a couple of sturdy cardboard books in the car for him to read as you drive along. Point out large, simple printed signs and other things of interest as you drive. Select books to read which include things your toddler has recently seen and experienced.

Send grandma or grandpa several of your child's favorite stories. Have the grandparent tape-record reading aloud several of the stories and mail the book and cassette back to you. Then watch your child's excitement as granny or grandpa reads to him!

Newspaper reading can be an enjoyable family activity, with each person reading a different section and the toddler getting the comics and the parts that everyone has finished with. Toddlers like to open the mail and "read" what is inside. Let her have the advertisements while you look at the important mail. Have each family member contribute a paragraph to a joint letter to send to a friend or relative and include the toddler's scribbles. Before sending it, read the combined message aloud to the whole family. Share short letters, favorite poems, or short passages from books at meal times.

Several authors writing about their families' reading patterns provide good evidence that reading naturally becomes a habit once the family takes the time to make it an important part of their routine.[9] In many cases reading aloud to the toddler begins the process of sharing literature among all the members of the family. Read-aloud sessions are respected in these families. Television takes a back seat. Once the pattern is established, reading and discussing books become as normal a part of daily living as eating, sleeping, and sports.

How Can We Develop Good Family Library Habits?

Your toddler loves to go to new places and see new things. Going "out" is a big treat. A trip to your public library or bookmobile can be pleasant for you both. Before your first visit to take out books for her, you might take time to explain what "borrowing" means so that she is not upset when the books must be returned later on.

Some libraries have begun toddler story hours or parent education classes for parents and their small children. These are especially worthwhile for sharing ideas with other parents.

Toddlers need to be closely supervised during library visits. Some parents (and librarians) worry about toddlers pulling books from shelves and tearing pages. You are the model for your child in the library. Take time to sit down and read a book. Let him see you doing it. Turn the pages gently. Talk softly. Your child will learn that this is the way to behave in the library. Copying you, he will select one book at a time to look at. When it is time to go, let your child take home several books and you take home several others. Then even if your child's choices are not suitable, yours will be. Your toddler will soon develop his own criteria for selecting books.

Librarians can be a big help in recommending books. Sometimes they will even take time to read a book with a toddler—a good positive encounter with another adult. Try to find at least one book dealing with some subject your toddler is currently interested in—cars, trucks, cows, clocks, or whatever she has noticed this week.

Physically, libraries can be very appealing to a toddler. There are often new stairs to climb, chairs to sit on, pictures and displays on the wall, and sometimes exhibits in cases, records to listen to, filmstrips to watch, and toys to play with.

Since books must be returned in two or three weeks, the library visit can become a pleasant routine. Unless you enjoy a major hunt every time books are due, it helps to store your library books in a special place separate from your own. Toddlers can learn to be responsible for their library books.

How Can I Involve My Toddler with Literature in Other Ways?

Toddlers like to be *doing*. With each book on the booklist that follows are suggestions for involving your toddler. Most toddlers like to sing, to pretend they are reading, to repeat things. Short rhymes and verses to accompany daily tasks are great fun. Try "Diddle, diddle dumpling, my son John," when one shoe is off and the other is on and "Rub-a-dub-dub" at bath time. Other rhymes and songs will occur to you during your child's day.

Walking and running are especially important to toddlers. They can act out, "Run, run, as fast as you can, you can't catch me, I'm the Gingerbread Man," or "Run little monkeys, run, run, run." One little child played a game with her father that they picked up from *The Gunniwolf*. She toddled away whispering "pit, pat," as her Dad followed her saying "hunkercha!" Another collected all the caps in the house, placed them on his head, and called, "Caps, caps for sale; fifty cents a cap," just as the peddler did in *Caps for Sale*. Most stories with any action can be acted out by a toddler, and finger plays and hand or finger puppets provide great fun.

As your toddler begins to say words, you will find she repeats short passages from books over and over again. Encourage this behavior by chanting along with your child. Make a picture book using magazine clippings of favorite objects. An easy way to do this is to buy an empty spiral-bound notebook of artists' sketch paper and paste pictures on each page. Family snapshot albums are fun for toddlers and help them learn people's names and remember past experiences.

Selected Booklist

Recommending specific titles for parents of toddlers is an imperfect art, since each toddler has his own special interests. Parents, with a librarian's help, can usually find situation books that their toddler will like because of the content. The following list contains some books that many toddlers have thoroughly enjoyed regardless of their specific interests. Either the illustrations are especially beautiful, or the language is lilting, or the story is a simple one with very few words on a page and an endearing central character, or the volume is an unusual size or shape, or the book begs for involvement. Since variety is important to your toddler, you will want to select some books from each category.

Tiny Books for Toddlers

There is something about tiny volumes (from three to six inches square) that makes them perfect for a toddler. Tiny fingers can turn the tiny pages. They are easy to pack for trips, fun to carry around the house and deposit in little nooks and crannies, ideal for reading independently in the car and elsewhere, and good for lap reading as well. If any book is especially suitable for the toddler age group, it is the tiny volume.

Carle, Eric. *My Very First Book of Colors*. New York:
Thomas Y. Crowell, 1974.
Older toddlers will enjoy matching the colors on the
top half of each page with the same-colored object
on the bottom half.

Coatsworth, Elizabeth. *Under the Green Willow*. Illus:
Jamina Domanske. New York: Macmillan, 1971.
Using only one or two words per page, ducks, fish,
and common animals gather under the green
willow. Good for animal sounds and for sequence.

Craig, Helen. *The Mouse House ABC*. New York: Random House, 1979.
Housed in a box, this alphabet book, with tiny,
dainty illustrations, unfolds into a long string of pictures. Most of the alphabet letters are part of a
picture—a hedge, a wall, etc. The illustrations are
really too adult for toddlers, but the size and shape
of the book make it appealing.

DeBrunhoff, Laurent. *Babar's Bookmobile; Babar's
Trunk*. New York: Random House.
Two boxed sets of tiny books (similar in format to
The Nutshell Library, below), each containing several Babar stories. Since these have quite a few
words on each page, they are for older toddlers, who
will grow to love the main character.

Lenski, Lois. *Little Train*. New York: Henry Z. Walck,
1940.
This is one of a series too numerous to describe individually. These volumes are distinctive because
of their precise vocabulary on subjects of great
interest to toddlers. Start with the *Little Train*, since
it is the simplest. The others have too many words
for a tiny toddler. Go on a little later to *Little
Airplane, Little Auto,* and *Little Farm*. The Small
family will become a part of yours as these volumes
catch on.

Potter, Beatrix. *The Tale of Peter Rabbit*. New York: Frederick Warne, 1902.

Some of the best literature in print today for any age group are the stories and poems of Beatrix Potter. The stories are best for older toddlers (age two and over) since there are too many words on some pages for the very little ones (though the stories can be paraphrased). The little rhyme books are for even the youngest toddlers. Each page has a few words with a small, clear and engaging picture.

Sendak, Maurice. *The Nutshell Library*. New York: Harper and Row, 1962.

Four tiny books: *Pierre; Alligators All Around; One was Johnny;* and *Chicken Soup with Rice.*

Rice is by far the best. *Alligators* and *Johnny* sound good, but toddlers can't make any sense out of them, and the moral of *Pierre* is far over their heads. Your toddler will be chanting "rice" at the end of each nonsensical line of *Chicken Soup with Rice*. You'll find yourself making chicken soup with rice for lunch. Fitting the volumes inside their little box is half the fun.

Songs, Rhymes, and Chants

You can capture a toddler's attention and keep it far longer if you sing or speak verse, rather than talk or read prose aloud. Songs and music have an attraction far beyond mere words. You'll want a song book, a poetry collection, several nursery rhyme or Mother Goose collections, and also books with individual songs or verses in them. The latter are especially appealing to a toddler because the verses go quickly, which means the pages can be turned rapidly. Play the music to these songs on a musical instrument and see if the child can guess the tune.

Recommendations for various Mother Goose collections appear in the infant chapter of this book. When selecting nursery rhymes for a toddler, try to find books that have a picture to match each rhyme. By the age of three, toddlers who have been reading Mother Goose since they were infants will be able to "read" many, many rhymes, if each rhyme has an illustration to cue them.

Blegvad, Lenore. *This Little Pig-a-Wig*. Illus: Eric Blegvad. New York: Atheneum, 1978.
Take your child to see some real pigs after reading these rhymes and stories.

Conover, Chris. *Six Little Ducks*. New York: Thomas Y. Crowell, 1976.
Visit a duck pond to sing this song. Your toddler will soon learn when to chime in on the "quack, quack, quack."

Garelick, May. *Where Does the Butterfly Go When It Rains?* Illus: Leonard Weisgard. Reading, Massachusetts: Addison-Wesley, 1961.
A beautiful poem with illustrations in light shades of blue. Read it when it is raining. It will stimulate your toddler's curiosity as well as her language.

Fisher, Aileen. *Once We Went on a Picnic*. Illus: Tony Chen. New York: Thomas Y. Crowell, 1975.
The rhymed story is delightful to hear, but the real fun is in trying to identify the 76 animals, birds, and plants that are illustrated in detailed color throughout the book. Fortunately for parents, there is a key on the last page!

———. *We Went Looking*. Illus: Marie Angel. New York: Thomas Y. Crowell, 1968.
One of the most visually appealing books in print, *We Went Looking* tells in rhyme how "we" looked

for a badger, but found all sorts of other animals. The toddler will learn the names of several different animals as well as some of the rhymes.

Langstaff, John. *Over in the Meadow*. Illus: Feodor Rojankovsky. New York: Harcourt Brace Jovanovich, 1967.

Wadsworth, Olive A. *Over in the Meadow*. Illus: Ezra Jack Keats. New York: Scholastic Book Services, 1971.

Although the illustrations are finer in the Rojankovsky edition, they are clearer and easier to count in the Keats edition; and your toddler will want to count after each verse. Read both. Your child will easily learn to rhyme the verses and will enjoy comparing the different versions of the song.

Kuskin, Karla. *A Boy Had a Mother Who Brought Him a Hat*. Boston: Houghton Mifflin, 1976.

Another short verse for a quick lap reading. The child will acquire visual discrimination skills as he tries to locate the red hat in each picture.

Langstaff, John. *Hot Cross Buns and Other Old Street Cries*. Illus: Nancy Winslow Parker. New York: Atheneum, 1978.

A delightful collection of easy rhymes and rounds from long ago.

———. *Oh, A-Hunting We Will Go*. Illus: Nancy Winslow Parker. New York: Atheneum, 1974.

After one reading (or singing) of this book a toddler will have fun completing some of the simpler rhymes before you turn the page to find the answer. This book has the advantage of including some advanced words, so interest in it will last a long time.

Bangs, Edward. *Steven Kellogg's Yankee Doodle*. Illus: Steven Kellogg. New York: Parents' Magazine Press, 1976.

Shackburg, Robert. *Yankee Doodle*. Illus: Ed Emberley. Englewood Cliffs, N.J.: Prentice-Hall, 1965.

These volumes will be as engaging for the parent as the toddler, since they contain such interesting information as the recipe for hasty pudding. Toddlers delight in singing the ten verses over and over again. Show your child a cannon, point out a stallion if you see one, make some hasty pudding. Play the music on a musical instrument and see if toddler can guess the tune.

Spier, Peter. *The Erie Canal*. Garden City, N.Y.: Doubleday, 1970.

Beautifully detailed pictures accompany the Erie Canal song. Act out the words—duck heads for the "low bridge," and recall the song when you see a bridge across a highway.

———. *London Bridge is Falling Down*. Garden City, N.Y.: Doubleday, 1967.

Not quite as interesting to a toddler as the *Erie Canal*, but longer—over 15 verses—and a toddler will want to hear every one of them. Play London Bridge next time there are several toddlers around.

Zemach, Margot. *Hush, Little Baby*. New York: E. P. Dutton, 1975.

Sing this lullaby before bed—or after tears.

Repetition

If toddlers could patent one word for their very own, that word would be "again." Repetition in stories, whether old or modern, is perfect for them. Many stories appear in several different versions. Some have better illustrations than others; some are more simply written; and some are less violent. Toddlers like to see and compare different versions of the same tale.

Emberley, Barbara. *Drummer Hoff*. Illus: Ed Emberley. Englewood Cliffs, N.J.: Prentice-Hall, 1967.

The cumulative, repetitive lines will encourage your toddler to complete the rhymes and chant, "And Drummer Hoff fired it off." Visit a cannon and play-act firing it. At a parade, point out the drummers. Let toddler play with a toy drum.

Arno, Ed. *The Gingerbread Man*. New York: Scholastic Book Services, 1967.

Galdone, Paul. *The Gingerbread Boy*. New York: Seabury, 1975.

The Scholastic version is the simpler of the two. It is more repetitious, and Scholastic has an accompanying phonograph record available. The Galdone illustrations are superior. Your child will chant, "Run, run, as fast as you can, You can't catch me, I'm the Gingerbread Man," while running around the house. Bake a gingerbread man, or buy one at a bakery, so that the idea of eating a gingerbread man is not frightening at the end. Lots of naming and pointing can accompany this story. You and your toddler can count the Gingerbread Man's buttons.

Galdone, Paul. *Three Bears*. Seabury, 1972. Paperback edition 1972.

This version is very simply written with lots of repetition. Help your child recognize the differences in size. Make some porridge for breakfast on a chilly morning.

———. *The Three Little Pigs*. New York: Seabury, 1970.

This version is very simply written, but the pigs get eaten. The version where they run to the next little pig's house might be more appropriate for some toddlers. Change voices when you read about the pigs and the wolf, and baby will "huff and puff" with you. Gather straw, sticks, and bricks so baby can play with them and build houses. This and the *Three Bears* help children learn the concept of the number "three."

Blair, Susan. *The Three Billy Goats Gruff.* New York: Scholastic Book Services, 1970.

Galdone, Paul. *The Three Billy Goats Gruff.* New York: Seabury, 1973.

Younger toddlers will try out "trip, trap, trip, trap," count the billy goats, and look for bridges. Older toddlers can learn to differentiate the goats' sizes and imitate the ugly troll. Use a different voice for each billy goat and for the troll when you read the book aloud.

Galdone, Paul. *The Little Red Hen.* New York: Seabury, 1973.

Holdsworth, W. *The Little Red Hen.* New York: Farrar, Straus and Giroux, 1968.

Lots of "Not I" responses match the negative talk toddlers love. Bake some bread and talk about where the flour came from, as the story does.

Harper, Wilhelmina. *The Gunniwolf.* Illus: William Wiesner. New York: E. P. Dutton, 1967.

For a very young toddler, this book can be the beginning of acting out a story. Encourage the child to "run" as you say, "hunkercha!" Little one will go, "Pit, pat." Toddler will sing along with "Kum-kwa, khi-wa." Provide several baskets of artificial flowers for picking or go out to pick some real ones and as you are picking sing, "Kum-kwa, khi-wa."

McGovern, Ann. *Stone Soup.* Illus: Nola Langner. New York: Scholastic Book Services, 1971.

Most toddlers love stones. They carry them around, store them, and play with them. The thought of making soup from a stone is funny even to them. They will memorize the order in which the ingredients were added to the pot and chant, "Soup from a stone, fancy that."

————. *Too Much Noise*. Illus: Simms Taback. Boston: Houghton Mifflin, 1967.

Lots of repeated sentences about a house that gets noisier before it gets quiet again give toddler practice in talking in sentences. Your child will enjoy making the animal sounds. Try this as a flannelboard story.

Slobodkina, Esphyr. *Caps for Sale*. Reading, Mass.: Addison-Wesley, 1947.

This will be near the top of your toddler's favorite list. He will repeat, "Caps. Caps for sale! Fifty cents a cap!" You'll both laugh at the monkeys' "Tsk, tsk." Gather a few caps together and let your child put them on and take them off while chanting. Point out the colors of the caps. When looking for something, have the child look to the right or to the left, as was done in the story, and chant, "No caps."

Soule, Jean C. *Never Tease a Weasel*. New York: Parents' Magazine Press, 1964.

Your toddler will chant, "But never tease a weasel; this is very good advice. A weasel will not like it, and teasing isn't nice." Count things on the pages, name the colors, or finish the rhymes with your child.

Involvement Books

In this section are books that are not read or sung aloud, but which are involvement books—books for pointing and naming things, alphabet and number books. These are books to move back and forth in, books that teach basic concepts, but have no story line.

Alexander, Anne. *ABC of Cars and Trucks*. Garden City,
    N.Y.: Doubleday, 1971.
    An alphabet book with a car or truck for each letter
    of the alphabet. This is a good book to take along on
    a drive and use to identify cars and trucks.
Ancona, George. *It's a Baby!* New York: E. P. Dutton,
    1979.
    The black and white photographs, which depict a
    baby's first year of life, are brilliant. Share this book
    with a toddler who is basking in the awareness that
    he is growing or with a toddler who is about to be-
    come a big sister or brother.
Anglund, Joan Walsh. *Emily and Adam* (three books in a
    case). New York: Random House, 1979.
    The case contains *The Adam Book, The Emily Book,
    and The Emily and Adam Book of Opposites*. Each
    is a very simple story of a child who has common,
    everyday experiences. In the book of opposites the
    point is made that even though Emily and Adam are
    opposite they are still the best of friends.
Aruego, José. *Look What I Can Do*. New York: Scrib-
    ner's, 1971.
    Copy what the animals do. See if your toddler can do
    what you do and then take your turn being a copycat.
    You can do exercises with your child this way.
Barrett, Judith. *Animals Should Definitely Not Wear
    Clothing*. Illus: Ron Barrett. New York: Atheneum,
    1970.
    Your toddler will laugh at the sight of animals in
    clothes. Leave some doll clothes near your child's
    stuffed animals and watch what happens. There is a
    great deal of word play in this book, which toddlers
    love.
Brimax Books. *Show Baby Opposites; Take a Long Look*.
    London: Brimax Books, 1973.

These series of simple cardboard books for children ages 2–4 are easy to handle and fun to talk about.

Brown, Marc. *One, Two, Three: An Animal Counting Book*. Boston: Little, Brown, 1976.

Toddlers not only learn to count the animals, but also learn both familiar and not-so-familiar animal names. Visit a zoo when reading this book.

Brown, Margaret Wise. *The Little Fireman*. Reading, Mass.: Addison-Wesley, 1952.

This has a story, but toddler will be more interested in finding two of everything and learning about big and little, and the colors red and green.

Carle, Eric. *Do You Want To Be My Friend?* New York: Thomas Y. Crowell, 1971.

Your toddler can guess from the tail of the animal in one picture what the animal on the next page will be. Another good book for helping toddlers learn to turn pages. It is also good for visual memory and discrimination.

———. *The Grouchy Ladybug*. New York: Thomas Y. Crowell, 1977.

Though a very young child will not grasp the story, there are an endless number of things to do with this book. The pages, of all different sizes, are easy to turn. The toddler can recognize and learn to say the names of each of the animals. The repetitive language patterns make good listening, and since there are few words on a page, the pages turn fast enough to sustain interest. Visually, the size of the ladybug, the size of the print, and the position of the sun changes on each page.

———. *The Very Hungry Caterpillar*. Cleveland: Collins-World, 1969.

Toddlers will enjoy this story, but will also have fun counting the things the caterpillar ate, learning the

days of the week, participating in the reading and
turning the pages of this interesting book with holes
for little fingers to push through.

Crowther, Robert. *The Most Amazing Hide-and-Seek
Alphabet Book*. New York: Viking, 1978.
Little cardboard flaps hide each animal. Watch your
child make the animals appear. She will learn the
names of all of them and call, "See!" when discovering another hidden animal. (Save this one for the
toddler who knows not to be rough with books.)

DeRegniers, Beatrice S. *It Does Not Say Meow*. Illus:
Paul Galdone. New York: Seabury, 1972.
Each riddle is answered by a lovely large, clear picture on the following page. In each case you and
your toddler can guess what the animal is. Point to
each letter in the word on the page with the picture
as you spell it. Make up more riddles.

Emberley, Ed. *Ed Emberley's A. B. C.* Boston: Little,
Brown, 1978.
The upper case letters are fun for the toddler to con-
nect with the pictured objects.

Ets, Marie Hall. *Just Me*. New York: Viking, 1965.
Your toddler will enjoy imitating the little boy in the
story who walks like each animal he encounters.

Fujikawa, Gyo. *Gyo Fujikawa's A to Z Picture Book*.
New York: Grosset and Dunlap, 1974.
This large-sized picture book includes all sorts of
things for a child to talk about—animals, babies, vehicles, and many common and not-so-common
items. It is a book that will be enjoyed for several
years. Older toddlers will pick up initial consonant
sounds from the pictures.

———. *Oh, What a Busy Day*. New York: Grosset and
Dunlap, 1976.
Also contains delightful illustrations of many every-
day events in a child's life. The questions and com-

ments they arouse will stimulate language development in your toddler.

⸻. *Our Best Friends*. New York: Grosset and Dunlap, 1977.

One in a series of cardboard books with delightful illustrations for toddlers to talk about. Although some of the titles are most suitable for infants, some, such as *Let's Eat, Our Best Friends, Sleepytime,* and *Surprise, Surprise,* all with animals as main characters, will please children in the toddler age group.

Garelick, May. *Down to the Beach*. Illus: Barbara Cooney. New York: Four Winds Press, 1973. Paperback edition, 1973.

Ideal adjunct to a beach visit. Your toddler can learn the names of different kinds of boats, fish, shells, and birds. Building a sand castle, or burying Daddy in sand are some of the activities this book will suggest.

Hutchins, Pat. *Clocks and More Clocks*. New York: Macmillan, 1970.

This is another book not written for toddlers but which appeals to them because they are challenged to find the clocks on each page, an activity that helps develop their visual discrimination. The clocks can be counted easily. "More" is also one of a toddler's favorite words and this book provides it. Visit a clock shop after reading this one and talk about all the different kinds of clocks.

⸻. *Changes, Changes*. New York: Macmillan, 1971.

Using no text, blocks are pictured to form a number of things, including a fire engine to put out a fire. Keep this one next to the blocks for reading when block play becomes monotonous.

Johnson, John E. *My School Book*. New York: Random House, 1979.

The first day of school is depicted in this cardboard

spiral-bound book. You might read this before your child goes to nursery school or day care for the first time and then compare your child's experiences with those in the book.

Kellogg, Stephen. *The Mystery of the Missing Red Mitten*. New York: Dial Press, 1974.

Toddlers have fun following the red mitten through the story and guessing where it will next be found. The text is too advanced, but the story can easily be paraphrased. The small size of the book invites your toddler to look at it alone after you have shared it together. Best read in wintertime.

Krauss, Ruth. *Is This You?* Illus: Crockett Johnson. New York: Scholastic Book Services, 1968.

Another "No" book toddlers will enjoy for its simple, funny illustrations. You can count and talk about things in the pictures.

Maestro, Betsy and Giulio. *On the Go: A Book of Adjectives*. New York: Crown, 1979.

This book is a bit didactic. It illustrates twenty-nine adjectives, such as "sad," "full," "hungry."

McMillan, Bruce. *The Remarkable Riderless Runaway Tricycle*. Boston: Houghton Mifflin, 1978.

Clear black-and-white photos tell, without words, the story of a discarded trike which eventually returns to its owner. Any child who has outgrown a loved toy will enjoy reading this book. Go out and ride trikes after reading it.

Moore, Lilian. *My Big Golden Counting Book*. Illus: Garth Williams. New York: Golden Press, 1957.

One of the most enjoyable counting books available, and one that your toddler will love having read aloud. It has little rhymes for each picture and clearly countable items. Stop after each rhyme to point and count the items, the child will soon copy you. The front end paper shows all the numbers, all mixed up. The child will have fun picking them out.

Munari, Bruno. *Bruno Munari's Zoo.* Cleveland: Collins-World, 1963.

The illustrations in this book are ideal for a toddler and make it perfect for reading before or after a zoo visit. The words are clever enough to entertain the parent as well. Toddler can learn to recognize the sign "Zoo" at the beginning and "Exit" at the end.

Petie, Haris. *A Book of Big Bugs.* Englewood Cliffs, N.J.: Prentice-Hall, 1977.

This is an example of an adult book, or at least one for junior high age or older, that can be enjoyed by a toddler because of its pictures. The words are all on the left-hand page and the pictures on the right. You can read the words while your toddler talks about the pictures. Bugs appeal to toddlers, and this book may interest you as well.

Piatti, Celestino. *Celestino Piatti's Animal ABC.* New York: Atheneum, 1966.

Although the illustrations are somewhat bold, your toddler will have fun finding the page that shows an animal you name.

Provensen, Alice and Martin. *Peaceable Kingdom: The Shaker Abecedarius.* New York: Viking, 1978.

Shaker children supposedly learned letters by singing this delightful alphabet song of animals. Each animal is pictured clearly from left to right across the page. The tune is that of the well-known ABC song. You'll find yourself singing this one in the shower. Don't miss it.

Rey, Hans A. *Anybody at Home?; Feed the Animals; See the Circus.* Boston: Houghton Mifflin, 1956.

Each page of these delightful books folds out to reveal a surprise inside—great for guessing and learn-

ing animal names and animal homes. These volumes make excellent books for a toddler to sit and
"read" alone.

Rice, Eve. *Sam Who Never Forgets*. New York: Greenwillow, 1977.

A story that will entertain toddlers and teach them to
identify each animal. They will learn which foods
each animal eats, point to balloons which appear on
each page, count them, and learn their colors. (The
balloons are in subtle shades of color that are not
easy to identify.) Another good book to use just before or after a zoo visit.

Richter, Mischa. *Quack?* New York: Harper & Row,
1978.

Duck goes through the book and says, "Quack" to
each animal and each responds with a different
sound. An enjoyable way for a toddler to learn the
sounds animals make. Try taking turns being the
duck and letting your toddler be the other animal,
and vice versa. Visit a duck pond after reading this
one.

Robinson, *The Ladybird ABC*. London: Loughborough,
1961.

The whole Ladybird series is excellent, but this one
and *A First Ladybird Key Words Dictionary* are
especially good for learning words. The *ABC* has
one picture per page, each of a very common object,
though several are clearly British. The small size of
the books makes them good car books.

Ruben, Patricia. *Apples to Zippers: An Alphabet Book*.
Garden City, N.Y.: Doubleday, 1976.

The clear photographs are easily recognizable by a
toddler. It is fun to find the objects pictured and to
learn the letters of the alphabet at the same time.

Shaw, Charles G. *It Looked Like Spilt Milk*. New York:
Harper & Row, 1947.

Silhouettes of common things are easy for the toddler to identify. He can answer, "No," when you ask, "Was it spilt milk?" In the end, the shape is discovered to be a cloud. Read this on a cloudy day and then go out to find shapes in the clouds.

Spier, Peter. *Gobble Growl Grunt*. Garden City, N.Y.: Doubleday, 1971.

All kinds of animals are depicted making their characteristic sounds, and you will imitate them as you read this with your toddler.

Tanz, Christine. *An Egg Is to Sit On*. Illus: Rosekrans Hoffman. New York: Lothrop, Lee and Shepard, 1978.

For older toddlers. "An egg is to sit on," the book begins. Turn the page and find, "if you are a chicken." The text will arouse children's curiosity and have them guessing what the "if" is. A good book for encouraging page turning.

Weihs, Erika. *Count the Cats*. Garden City, N.Y.: Doubleday, 1976.

The illustrations in this book are very colorful, making it great for pointing things out and talking about them. Name the colors and count the cats on each page.

Winter, Paula. *The Bear and the Fly*. New York: Crown, 1976.

For the toddler who is familiar with swatting flies with a fly swatter the humor in this wordless small book will be appropriate. You'll have to point out the fly swatter at first, because only the handle shows in some of the illustrations.

Wynne, Patricia. *The Animal ABC*. New York: Random House, 1977.

This delightful cardboard book has very clear color illustrations of animals, both familiar and less well-known, for each letter of the alphabet. An ideal time

to present this book to your child is just after she has
acquired alphabet blocks. The toddler will begin to
associate an animal with each letter of the alphabet
(a prereading skill). You can also talk about the features of various animals: tails, wings, and four legs.
Because the book is cardboard, the child can be allowed to "read" it independently in places like the
car.

Storybooks

Few authors write storybooks for very young children.
Marjorie Flack is one of the few whose books are perfect
for this age group. However, some books written for
older children can be used with toddlers if their story
line sustains the child's interest. Such books usually
have one central character who can be followed through
the book, a picture of that character on each page, very
few words on a page, clear illustrations accompanying
the text, and a relatively simple story line.

Adams, Adrienne L. *A Woggle of Witches*. New York:
    Scribner's, 1971.
    This might seem an unlikely title to include in a
    toddler reading list, but the story is delightful and
    the illustrations are different enough to provide real
    entertainment for your toddler. You'll enjoy talking
    about "spiderweb bread," and "bat stew." The tod-
    dler will supply the "Zoom . . ." and "Whee . . ."
    sound effects and identify the children in Hallo-
    ween costumes.
Allamand, Pascale. *The Little Goat in the Mountains*.
    New York: Frederick Warne, 1978.
    The little goat is saved from danger in the mountains
    and returns to the village with a lovely garland of

flowers. The concept of herding might be related to any experiences your child has had with cows or goats.

Allen, Frances C. *Little Hippo.* Illus: Laura J. Allen. New York: G. P. Putnam, 1971.
Little Hippo misses his Mother when she is taken away to have a baby. This very short book can be read to very little toddlers when Mother (or another adult they know) has a new baby.

Bornstein, Ruth. *Little Gorilla.* New York: Seabury, 1976.
In this very short book Little Gorilla grows as his family looks on. If you keep a wall chart of your toddler's growth, this might be a good book to share just before measuring toddler's new height.

Brown, Margaret Wise. *Country Noisy Book.* Illus: Leonard Weisgard. New York: Harper & Row, 1940, Paperback edition, 1976.
You and your toddler will enjoy taking turns making the noises in this book as well as listening for noises in your neighborhood. If you take a trip from the city to the country or vice versa you can talk about the changes in the noises you hear.

———. *Noisy Book.* Illus: Leonard Weisgard. New York: Harper & Row, 1939.
Similar to the previous book, you can enjoy noticing sounds after reading this book.

———. *The Runaway Bunny.* Illus: Clement Hurd. New York: Harper & Row, new edition, 1972. Paperback edition, 1977.
Toddler helps the mother bunny find the baby bunny in the pictures and enjoys the repetitive language.

Burningham, John. *Mr. Gumpy's Motor Car.* New York: Thomas Y. Crowell, 1976.
The appealing animals in this story meet a crisis and

end up splashing into the water. Your toddler will enjoy doing his own splashing.

Burton, Virginia Lee. *The Little House*. Boston: Houghton Mifflin, 1942. Paperback edition, 1978.

The house is the main character in this story. At first you can just tell the story in your own words while the toddler points out the minute details in the pictures. Later he will enjoy listening to the story. You can point out all sorts of different houses as you are driving in the car. You can also talk about the book as you ride an elevated railroad, a subway, or a streetcar.

————. *Mike Mulligan and His Steam Shovel*. Boston: Houghton Mifflin, 1939. Paperback edition, 1977.

Toddlers love to visit construction sites and watch the heavy equipment, so even though earth movers are no longer powered by steam, Mike remains a popular toddler hero.

Flack, Marjorie. *Angus and the Cat*. Garden City, N.Y.: Doubleday, 1931.

Angus, a Scottie dog, searches all over for the cat who moved in with him. Toddler will have fun finding the cat in the picture and seeing how the two become friends in the end. This book would especially appeal to children who have pets.

————. *Ask Mr. Bear*. New York: Macmillan, 1958.

This is the most delightful book available for a toddler. Danny seeks a present for his mother from all of the animals; there is lots of repetition. Mother guesses and Danny replies, "No," to each guess— fun for toddlers who like to say, "No." A bear hug makes a delightful way to end the story reading.

Freeman, Don. *Beady Bear*. New York: Viking, 1954. Paperback edition, 1977.

A long story with very few words on a page and

black and white woodcut illustrations, this book tells of a windup bear who comes alive. Let your toddler hold a teddy, especially if you have a wind-up one.

————. *Corduroy*. New York: Viking, 1968. Paperback edition, 1976.

For toddlers who like teddy bears, Corduroy will have immediate appeal. Make a bed from a box for your child's teddy bear or read the story after sewing on a button. When you ride an escalator remind toddler about Corduroy. Get teddy to listen to the story with your toddler.

————. *A Rainbow of my Own*. New York: Viking, 1966. Paperback edition, 1974.

The boy in this story dreams about playing with a rainbow of his own and then finds one in his goldfish bowl. You might read this after seeing a rainbow. Or provide a prism to find rainbows of your own.

Ginsburg, Mirra. *Mushroom in the Rain*. New York: Macmillan, 1974.

Suteyev, A. *Mushroom in the Rain*. Illus: José Aruego. New York: Macmillan, 1974.

Everyone knows what happens to a mushroom in the rain. It grows! That's why so many animals can fit underneath it. Either version of this clever story will have you and your toddler watching toadstools grow.

Haas, Irene. *The Maggie B*. New York: Atheneum, 1975.

This is one of the most delightful books ever written. Its story is lively—small brother is a very nice boy instead of the bothersome pest that little brothers are in most books. The illustrations are warm and delicate; the language is beautiful; and several songs are included. Don't miss sharing this one with your toddler. Find some boats or pictures of boats and point out their names; sit in a rocking chair and rock as though you were in a boat.

Hutchins, Pat. *Rosie's Walk*. New York: Macmillan, 1968. Paperback edition, 1971.
A very simple text tells of Rosie the hen and her walk through the barnyard, where she is stalked by a fox and meets with every comic disaster imaginable. Even toddlers see the humor in the story.

Keats, Ezra Jack. *The Snowy Day*. New York: Viking, 1962.
Read this one in the wintertime when there is snow on the ground. Make snowballs and play with sticks, as in the story.

————. *Whistle for Willie*. New York: Viking, 1964. Paperback edition, 1977.
Many commonplace objects appear in the story: a traffic light, a dog, a hat, a shopping bag. Peter jumps—can the toddler jump?

Krauss, Robert. *Herman the Helper*. Illus: José Aruego and Arianne Dewey. New York: E. P. Dutton, 1974.
Herman, an octopus, helps everyone, but he helps himself to the mashed potatoes. The toddler can try "helping." Animals, balloons, and bright colors provide lots of opportunity for involvement.

————. *Whose Mouse Are You?* New York: Macmillan, 1970. Paperback edition, 1972.
Use the simple illustrations to point out ears, eyes, nose, whiskers, claws and teeth. Follow the mouse through the book. Soon the toddler will be able to answer the questions the story asks.

Krauss, Ruth. *The Happy Day*. Illus: Marc Simont. New York: Harper & Row, 1949.
This very simple story has bears, squirrels, groundhogs, and snails who run, jump, and find the first flower of spring!

————. *The Happy Egg*. New York: Scholastic Book Services, 1972.

A very simple story with one color—blue—for the
egg that hatches into a bird. Your toddler will be
"reading" this one on his own very quickly. The
sounds, "POP" and "peep" give clues to the action.

Kroll, Steven. *If I Could Be My Grandmother*. Illus:
Lady McCrady. New York: Pantheon, 1977.

Grandparents are important to toddlers and there
are few books for toddlers about their grandmothers.
The role of the mother in this story is not a good one,
but the story of grandmother's visit, after a girl pretends to be grandmother with her dolls, will involve
a child. See if your toddler starts playing grandmother to dollies.

La Fontaine. *The Lion and the Rat*. Illus: Brian Wildsmith. New York: Franklin Watts, 1963.

The characters in this book make the story appropriate for a toddler.

Lasker, Joe. *Lentil Soup*. Chicago: Albert Whitman,
1977.

The front of the book tells you that the book is about
relationships between two people, the numbers one
through seven, order, and the days of the week, so
you already know that a lot can be learned from this
story. It's also fun to make lentil soup after reading
this one.

Lionni, Leo. *Alexander and the Wind-Up Mouse*. New
York: Pantheon, 1969. Paperback edition, 1974.

You can point out likenesses and differences between the real mouse and the windup mouse. If
baby has a toy mouse, the book will be especially
appealing. A good time to read this book is when the
toddler has just learned how to wind things up.

————. *Inch by Inch*. New York: Astor-Honor, 1962.

The inchworm is the central character and it is fun to

find him on each page. The toddler can learn the
bird names and count to five with the inchworm.

―――. *Frederick*. New York: Pantheon, 1966. Paperback edition, 1966.

Although they will miss the point of the story,
toddlers will enjoy finding Frederick on each page
and talking about how he is different from the other
mice.

―――. *Swimmy*. New York: Pantheon, 1963.

Swimmy can be identified on each page as you read
his adventures aloud. You might visit an aquarium
store to see different kinds of fish after reading
Swimmy.

Littledale, Freya. *The Elves and the Shoemaker*. Illus:
Brinton Turkle. New York: Scholastic Book Services, 1977.

This nice, calm story about shoes presents tiny elves
that are like children. Visit a shoemaker or shoestore
and talk about all the different kinds of shoes after
reading this book.

Lukesova, Milena. *Julian in the Autumn Woods*. Illus:
Jan Kudlacek. New York: Holt, Rinehart and
Winston, 1977.

Julian finds a chestnut while watching the falling
leaves. In the fall when toddler enjoys playing in the
leaves perhaps you, too, can find a chestnut.

Nakatani, Chiyoko. *My Day on the Farm*. New York:
Thomas Y. Crowell, 1977.

This very simple story, written in the first person, is
ideal for reading before bedtime, for it goes from the
morning to the night of one day on a farm. It would
be fun to read after visiting a farm. Children can
identify the animals in it.

Orbach, Ruth. *Apple Pigs*. Cleveland: Collins-World,
1977.

Toddlers will need help getting the message, which is about cleaning up, but they will need no help in discovering that the apple tree is overloaded. You can talk about the many things you can do with apples—and then do them.

Preston, Edna M. *Where Did My Mother Go?* Illus: Chris Conover. New York: Scholastic Book Services, 1978.

Baby cat looks for Mother in a supermarket, a laundromat, a service station, a library, and a shopping center, and finds her at home. Toddlers may not understand the story, nor is it wise for them to hear that others will not help search for Mother, but the familiar places that can be talked about, the repetitive language, and the "Not I" response of each person (reminding toddler of *Little Red Hen*) will make the book appealing.

Turkle, Brinton. *Thy Friend Obadiah*. New York: Viking, 1969.

A boy in a Quaker family befriends a seagull who has been following him around. This would be a good story to accompany helping any animal in trouble. The sequels, *Obadiah the Bold* and *Rachel and Obadiah* are also beautiful stories.

Notes

[1] Orvis C. Irwin, "Infant Speech: Effect of Systematic Reading of Stories." *Journal of Speech and Hearing Research*, 3 (June 1960) p. 187–190.

[2] Annis Duff, *"Bequest of Wings" A Family's Pleasures with Books* (New York: Viking, 1944) p. 17.

[3] Phyllis Fenner, *Something Shared: Children and Books* (New York: John Day, 1959) p. 19.

[4] Duff, p. 17.

[5] Julie M. T. Chan, *Why Read Aloud to Children?* an IRA Micromonograph. (Newark, Delaware: International Reading Association, 1974).

[6] Burton L. White, *The First Three Years of LIFE* (Englewood Cliffs, N.J.: Prentice-Hall, 1975).

[7] James E. Flood, "Parental Styles in Reading Episodes with Young Children." *The Reading Teacher*, 30 (May 1977) p. 864–867.

[8] May L. Becker, First Adventures in Reading: *Introducing Children to Books* (New York: F. A. Stokes, 1936).

[9] Lela Berg, *Reading and Loving* (London: Heineman, 1976). Annis Duff, *"Bequest of Wings"* A *Family's Pleasures with Books* (New York: Viking, 1944) p. 17. Phyllis Fenner, *Something Shared: Children and Books* (New York: John Day, 1959) p. 19. D. White, *Books Before Five* (London: Oxford University Press, 1954).

References

Becker, May L. *First Adventures in Reading: Introducing Children to Books*. New York: F. A. Stokes, 1936.

Berg, Lela. *Reading and Loving*. London: Heineman, 1976.

Chan, Julie M. T. *Why Read Aloud to Children?* an IRA Micromonograph. Newark, Delaware: International Reading Association, 1974.

Duff, Annis. *"Bequest of Wings" A Family's Pleasures with Books*. New York: Viking, 1944.

Fenner, Phyllis. *Something Shared: Children and Books*. New York: John Day, 1959.

Flood, James E. "Parental Styles in Reading Episodes with Young Children," *The Reading Teacher*, 30 (May 1977).

Irwin, Orvis C. "Infant Speech: Effect of Systemic Reading of Stories" *Journal of Speech and Hearing Research*, 3 (June 1960).

Rogers, Norma. *How Can I Help My Child Get Ready to Read?* an IRA Micromonograph. Newark, Delaware: International Reading Association, 1972.

White, Burton L. *The First Three Years of LIFE*. Englewood Cliffs, N.J.: Prentice-Hall, 1975.

White, D. *Books Before Five*, New York: Oxford University Press, 1954.

III

Sharing Literature with Your Prereader

Ages 3—5

Did you have a favorite picture book before you went to school? Do you remember sitting on your father's or mother's lap as the book was read to you? Will your preschool child have similar memories?

Most parents recognize that a child's home environment during the preschool years critically influences later achievement and attitudes. More specifically, the first five years of a child's life are highly important in the formation of language development, prereading skills, and attitudes about literature. As a parent you play the most important role in the sharing of literature with your prereader, because only you share the intimate relationship with your child special to the natural or surrogate parent. No teacher or friend of later childhood will ever have as great an influence with the child as you now have in this regard. Therefore, in your attitude toward books and what you do with them, you provide a vital role model for your child. Given a stimulating home environment where many books have been shared in a warm, comfortable atmosphere, children are much more likely to go to school eager to learn to read, confident about their ability to do so, and excited about books.

But even though you want to share interesting books with your young child, getting him and these books together is a real challenge. Not only are there many other demands on your time, but television competes relentlessly for the child's time and attention. This chapter will give you some practical suggestions and guidelines that should help you select and share appropriate books of quality with your prereading child. We have left the age at which a toddler becomes a preschooler open. You may find recommendations given in the toddler chapter or the beginning reader chapter more appropriate for your own child, but in general this chapter focuses on children from 3 to 5 years old.

What Is Good Literature for a Prereader?

The books you share with your prereader should be of high quality. Because there are so many books available to choose from, it is necessary to be selective in the choices you make. And exactly how do you know which books are best?

There are two general guidelines that you may find helpful in selecting good books to share with your prereading child:

1. Does the book match the child's needs and interests?

2. Are both the art work and the text of the book of high quality? Considering the first guideline, we might now ask, what are the needs and interests of preschool children? The following broad characteristics of 3-, 4-, and 5-year-old children dictate appropriate book suggestions for prereaders.

LITERATURE FOR PREREADERS**

Characteristics	Implications	Examples*
Rapid development of language.	Interest in words, enjoyment of rhymes, nonsense and repetition and cumulative tales. Enjoys retelling folktales and stories from books without words.	*Mother Goose* *Millions of Cats* *The Three Bears* *Drummer Hoff* *Deep in the Forest*
Very active, short attention span.	Requires books that can be completed "in one sitting." Enjoys participation through naming, touching, and pointing.	*The Very Hungry Caterpillar* *Who's there? Open the Door!*

LITERATURE FOR PREREADERS**

Characteristics	Implications	Examples*
	Should have the opportunity to hear stories several times each day.	
Child is the center of the world: interest, behavior and thinking are egocentric.	Likes characters with which she can clearly identify. Can only see one point of view.	*Bedtime for Frances* *The Snowy Day* *Nobody Asked Me If I Wanted a Baby Sister*
Curious about the world around him.	Enjoys stories about everyday experiences, pets, playthings, home, people in his immediate environment.	*Peter's Chair* *William's Doll*
Building concepts through many firsthand experiences.	Uses books with activities that extend and reinforce developing concepts.	*Count and See* *Push, Pull, Empty, Full*

LITERATURE FOR PREREADERS**

Characteristics	*Implications*	*Examples**
Child has little sense of time. Time is "before now," "now," and "not yet."	Can get help from books in beginning to understand the sequence of time.	*Seasons* *It's Time Now* *Winter's Coming*
Child learns through imaginative play.	Enjoys stories that involve imaginative play. Likes personification of toys and animals.	*May I Bring a Friend?* *How Santa Had a Long and Difficult Journey Delivering His Presents*
Seeks warmth and security in relationships with adults.	Likes to be close to the teacher or parent during story time. The ritual of the bedtime story is a way to make the experience of literature part of the daily routine.	*Goodnight Moon* *Ask Mr. Bear*
Beginning to assert inde-	Books that reflect child's	*The Runaway Bunny* *The Carrot Seed*

LITERATURE FOR PREREADERS**

Characteristics	*Implications*	*Examples**
pendence. Takes delight in own accomplishments.	own emotions.	*Ira Sleeps Over* *There's a Nightmare in My Closet*
Beginning to make value judgments about what is fair and what should be punished.	Requires poetic justice and happy endings in the stories.	*Titch* *The Tale of Peter Rabbit* *The Three Pigs* *Snow-White and the Seven Dwarfs*

*See the booklist, pp. 81, for authors' names and other details about the suggested books.
**Adapted from chart in Huck, Charlotte S. *Children's Literature in the Elementary School*, 3rd ed. New York: Holt, Rinehart and Winston, 1976, 31–32.

May Hill Arbuthnot, an authority in the area of children's literature, believes that children have several basic needs—they need security, love, competence, belonging, variety, and beauty. In her book, *Reading in the Home*, she states that literature helps meet these needs because, "In children's books these needs—for security, for love, for competence, for belonging, for change, and for beauty and harmony—supply the motivating forces that spark the action of the characters."[1] Thus, when a child identifies with a character in a book, he can better understand himself and others.

The second major consideration in choosing a good book is to evaluate the quality of the text (how language is used) and the illustrations. The text of a superior children's book has the same qualities as that of a superior adult book: well-drawn characters, an important theme, a lively plot, and an appealing style. The language should be precise, appropriate, colorful, descriptive, rich, and unrestricted. Not all the books you pick will live up to every one of these requirements, but you'll want to think about them as you select books to read with your child.

The best illustrations are those that are interesting, attractive, and enjoyable, and that promote a love of beauty. Both the illustrations and the text should portray sincere human emotions, warmth, and a positive outlook upon which the child can build.

Some of the questions you might ask as you evaluate the illustrations of a book are:

1. Does the picture accurately interpret the text? For example, if the story is about seven princesses the illustration should show all seven princesses; some other number would be confusing to the young "reader." People and objects should be shown in correct proportion to one another.

2. Are the pictures synchronized with the text? It is best that they appear on the same page as the part of the story they illustrate.

3. Do the pictures have interesting action?

4. Are colors bright? Although children generally prefer colors, however, they also enjoy illustrations in muted tones or black and white when the pictures are well done. For example, Robert McCloskey's books: *Blueberries for Sal, Make Way for Ducklings,* and *One Morning in Maine,* aren't in color, but the illustrations are still very appealing.

5. Are the illustrations of good quality? Do they have depth, tone, and other artistic values?

Other things to consider:

1. Does the book have a sturdy binding, good quality paper, and an appealing format?

2. Do *you* like it? It is best to share only those books that you genuinely like.

But what about the inexpensive books often available in grocery and drug stores? Some of these have poor illustrations and contrived storylines. Is it really important that young children have high-quality illustrations? Although children will accept poorly done pictures if the story is good, it is well to remember that the early experiences with art that children have will guide and sensitize them to an appreciation of art later in their lives and may help them develop a more discerning eye and taste.

A final suggestion for choosing literature for pre-readers is to include many different types of books: Mother Goose books, alphabet books, counting books, concept books, and storybooks. Specific examples of each of these types of books will be found in the selected booklist at the end of this chapter.

Using the criteria and guidelines mentioned in this section, you can select the right books for your child from the many available. And one way you'll know that your choice was right is when you finish reading a book to your child and she says enthusiastically, "Read it again!"

How Do I Read Aloud with My Preschool Child?

When your child sits close to you or on your lap and hears you read a book he benefits not only from the exposure to quality literature but also from the warmth, love, and closeness of this special relationship with you. Here are seven excellent tips based on Nancy Larrick's book, *A Parent's Guide to Children's Reading*—tips that will make this read-aloud time special:[2]

1. Plan ahead. Choose a time when there will be no interruptions from the telephone or television (turn them off if you need to). If possible, have a regular time each day to read together.

2. Select a place that will be quiet and comfortable, such as a bedroom or a quiet spot outdoors. Sit so your child can see the pictures easily; most children will enjoy being in your lap or very near you.

3. Before story time, select several books you think your child will enjoy. It is best to read through the stories and rhymes you plan to use before sharing them so that you can read them smoothly. You may even wish to record yourself on tape to see how your voice will sound to others.

4. Try to read in a natural voice, neither "sweet" nor condescending, but soft, low, and interested.

5. Begin with the familiar. You might want to say a Mother Goose rhyme that you have chosen, or that your child picked out herself. Let her join in if she wants to.

6. Pause at intervals to give the child a chance to comment. After a book has been read several times you may want to talk with her about the story and pictures, but do not be surprised if she doesn't want to interrupt the reading for questions or comments.

7. Respect your child's mood. If he is bored or restless, perhaps the book or the time is not right. If he doesn't want to discuss the pictures, step up the pace. If he wants to turn several pages to finish a book more quickly, let him. If he would rather go off and play, let him and wait to read until he is more responsive.

As you read aloud you might help your child along in acquiring reading readiness skills. Your child is beginning to develop *auditory discrimination*—the ability to make finer distinctions in the sounds she hears. This is one of the skills that indicates reading readiness. You can help by reading rhyming literature and by encouraging the child to join in the rhyming. Another skill your child will learn is to identify words that start with the same sounds, for example, in the titles of *Max the Mouse*, and *Moving Molly*.

Along with the ability to discriminate sound comes the reading readiness skill called *visual discrimination*. First, the child learns to discriminate colors, sizes, and shapes, which you can point out as you read. Later, he will begin to discriminate letters and words. Before you begin the book, point to the words in the title as you read them. See if your child can find those words later in the text of the story. You won't want to point all the time to each word as you read, but if a particular word stands out (such as a character's name) or if your child shows interest in a certain word, it is a good idea to point. For example, in *Where the Wild Things Are*, Max's name can be found in the text and on the picture of the boat also.

It might be wise, at this time, to have your child's sight evaluated. Parents are often not aware of eye problems until the child has suffered a long period of frustrating difficulties with reading that could, with knowledge, have been avoided.

Another reading readiness skill (called *metalinguistic awareness*) is learning that printed language must make sense, and has consistent rules, such as that we move from left to right in reading and writing, and that speech may be duplicated on paper; ink on paper may become speech. Here you can help your child by encouraging her to turn pages while you are reading aloud, to look at books independently and perhaps to listen to a tape of a story while following along in a book. You might talk to your child about authors and illustrators, point to words you read aloud, and make simple books that your child can illustrate.

The final reading readiness skill is having *a sense of story*. As you read aloud a wide variety of literature, your child learns all sorts of things about story plots, character development, sequence of events, cause and effect—all of the elements present in the stories you are reading. When she has memorized a story and "reads" it by looking at the pictures, she is developing a sense of story.

Once again, the goal of sharing literature with your child is not to teach your child how to read. But, if you read a variety of literature frequently and well, you can be sure that your child is acquiring reading readiness skills that will help him learn to read more easily.

How Do I Create a Stimulating Home Reading Environment?

There are several things you can do to create the kind of home environment that will encourage your preschool child to develop good reading habits, skills, and attitudes. First, you yourself should be a model for the child by having books around the house and by reading yourself. Your example and personal enthusiasm will influence your child.

Next, provide a place for your child's "home library" books, whether these are books that have been borrowed or books your child owns. Place some of these books face out on the shelf, with the colorful jackets showing.

Third, schedule a regular time each day in a quiet place for reading and looking at books, so that your child anticipates this time together. Probably, you will also have to schedule wisely the time that your preschooler spends watching television so that there will be time to include books. When given a choice, most young children jump at a chance to be read to—even when there is a competing television program.

Fourth, help your child acquire her own library by giving books as gifts, and encouraging grandparents and others to do the same. Fortunately, many high-quality books are now available in an inexpensive paperback edition in addition to the hardcover version. You can also take your child to bookstores and to the public library, so that you and she may select books together either to buy (with gift money, for instance) or to borrow.

How Can Our Family Develop Good Family Reading Habits?

As was mentioned in the previous section, adults who read each day and a good physical environment are important elements in a family reading program. Since reading aloud increases children's interest in books, it is important to spend time reading together each day. Some parents read to their preschoolers in the morning before or after breakfast, before the afternoon nap, or at bedtime. You may wish to check with your local library to see if they have a list of "cuddle books" for reading aloud to your preschooler.

Establishing family traditions involving literature will provide pleasant experiences now and happy memories later. For example, the father of one family read an Edgar Allan Poe story to his children and some of their neighborhood friends every Halloween when the children came back from "trick-or-treating." The reading was a ritual, set in the candle-lit living room. Another family read the Bible story of the first Christmas every year as they all gathered on Christmas Eve to spend this special evening together. Dickens's *A Christmas Carol* has been a read-aloud favorite with many families over the years.

You can often use books in conjunction with family vacations and outings. Go to the bookstore or library for a book about farm animals before you go for a drive in the country. There are many good picture books about nature that can precede or follow a trip to a wildlife center, a state park, or a zoo.

How Can Our Family Develop Good Family Library Habits?

One of the greatest resources you have is your public library or bookmobile, where you can borrow books and other materials. In addition to a central library building, which usually has a children's room, many libraries have bookmobiles that travel regularly to areas where library visits are difficult. These bookmobiles offer many of the same services that the central library does. Explore the services of your local library and then, if necessary, suggest that the library provide additional needed services.

There are a number of public library services that will interest and help you as the parent of a prereader. Library services that used to be available only to children attending school, such as story hours and vacation reading clubs, have recently been made available to preschoolers, as well as to hospitalized children, and the children of migrant workers.

Many libraries now have a story hour especially for preschoolers. Often these programs are multi-media presentations and children are involved in music, art, puppetry, films, flannelboard stories, science experiments and nature discussions in addition to the books themselves. Some libraries even have special hours such as "Sleepy-time Story Hours" or "PJ Stories" where children go in their pajamas in the evening, hear some stories and a lullaby, and then go home to bed.

The Provo Public Library in Provo, Utah, has extended its regular summer reading program to children of preschool age. The theme of one summer reading program was outer space, with appropriate pictures and models. Readers were awarded flags on a roster for books read; preschoolers shared in the awards by being allowed to count the stories read to them.

Some libraries also have a "Dial-a-Story" program, where a recorded poem or story for preschoolers is played over the telephone. Toy or media libraries where preschoolers may check out games, books, filmstrips, toys, and animal pets are becoming available. Some libraries even provide story hours in the homes of shut-in preschoolers. It would be well to find out which of these services are available at your local library, use those that meet your needs and those of your child, and help establish new programs that your community needs.

How Can I Involve My Preschool Child with Literature in Other Ways?

There are other ways to share literature with your child. You could invite a small group of neighbor children to your home regularly for a story hour. (It might be possible to alternate the responsibility for this hour with the other parents in the group.) You might also use television programs and movies to involve your child with books. If there is a television program or movie based on an appropriate book, share the book with your child before or after the viewing. Or select a book having the same topic or theme as a television program or movie.

Another inexpensive and simple activity would be to let your child write and make her own books. An alphabet book, number book, or book about your family would be good beginning topics. You could staple together your child's drawings, labeled by you, into a book. Pictures from magazines may be used as illustrations. A large, brown paper grocery sack doubled and sewn down the center on a sewing machine makes a durable book for the smallest child. An older preschooler could make covers for a book or from paper cardboard covered with wallpaper or contact paper. Spiral-bound sketch books with their thick paper pages are good for drawing and pasting. Your child can dictate stories to you or to older brothers and sisters. Children can dictate totally original stories after reading a book or make up sequels to their favorite stories.

Selected Booklist

The selection of books for this list is a subjective one but we have tried to balance the number of recently published books and those which are less recent. We chose books illustrated with a variety of art techniques, books that meet various needs and have diverse themes and settings, and books that are sensitive and unbiased in their treatment of cultures, groups, and roles appropriate for men and women.

As you look at the booklist that follows you might keep in mind the following statement from the American Library Association:

There is no magic in a book list that will guarantee a love of reading to any child. The magic is in the books themselves. When parents who have special knowledge concerning their own children work with teachers and librarians who know many books and many children, the finding of the right book is more likely to occur. Reading pleasure is made up of three parts—searching for the book, reading the book, and then sharing the book with someone else. Parents play a most important role in all three steps.

The best way to involve your child with these books is to look at and read them with him. Other activities for involvement, such as those that accompany the books listed below, might be appropriate after the book has been read aloud one or more times. They will help you "stretch" the book. You must be careful, however, to involve your child only in as many activities as will add to his enjoyment of the book, but not so many that he will become bored with it. Enjoyment of literature is your goal.

Books for Language Fun

You'll want to be sure to continue reading, chanting, and singing the nursery rhymes your child has enjoyed as an infant and toddler. In addition you'll want to branch out to books full of word play, more sophisticated alphabet books, and books of poetry.

Ahlberg, Janet and Allen. *Each Peach, Pear, Plum*. New
    York: Viking, 1978.
    "In this book with your little eye, take a look and
    play 'I spy'." Rhymes lead from one page to another.
Bayley, Nicola. *Nicola Bayley's Book of Nursery
    Rhymes*. New York: Alfred A. Knopf, 1977.

Because the detailed Victorian illustrations are too intricate for infants and toddlers, this makes an appropriate new nursery rhyme book for prereaders.

Burningham, John. *John Burningham's ABC*. Indianapolis: Bobbs-Merrill, 1967.

This alphabet book shows upper and lowercase letters and words beginning with the alphabet letter on the left-hand page and bold, simple pictures on the opposite page. It makes a good model for an ABC book you and your child can make.

Cohen, Miriam. *When Will I Read?* Illus: Lillian Hoban. New York: Greenwillow, 1977.

A very sensitive teacher points out to Jim that he already can read signs in the room. But Jim is not really reading until he notices that one sign has been changed. This book should give you and your prereader lots of ideas for making signs and writing stories together.

DeRegniers, Beatrice S. *May I Bring A Friend?* Illus: Beni Montresor. New York: Atheneum, 1964. Paperback edition, 1974.

The king and queen invite a little boy to come to tea—in rhyme. A child will find the friends from the zoo the boy brings with him very funny, and may give a tea party for his own stuffed animals.

Emberley, Ed. *Ed Emberley's ABC*. Boston: Little, Brown, 1978.

The humorous illustrations show animals engaged in a variety of activities and cleverly introduce the letters of the alphabet. In a sequence of four pictures across each page, the letter is presented; on the right-hand side of the page is a word with that letter in it. At the end of the book there's a chart showing how to form the capital letters and a list of objects to look for in the pictures. For the child who is beginning to write letters, this book provides a model.

Frost, Robert. *Stopping by Woods on a Snowy Evening.*
Illus: Susan Jeffers. New York: E. P. Dutton, 1978.
Susan Jeffers's illustrations make a picture book of
this well-known Frost poem. Her soft drawings of
wintry scenes, mostly in black and white, accompany each line of the poem, and bring to life a kindly
old man and his friends. Your child may want to
make "angels" in the snow or feed wildlife after
sharing this book.

Gag, Wanda. *Millions of Cats.* New York: Coward-
McCann and Geoghegan, 1928. Paperback edition,
1977.
This is a classic. Your child will easily memorize the
rhyming refrain in this absurd tale of a man who
brings home "millions, and billions, and trillions of
cats."

Galdone, Paul. *The Magic Porridge Pot.* New York: Seabury, 1976.
A girl must say the correct phrase to stop the porridge before it covers the tower.

————. *Old Mother Hubbard and Her Dog.* New York:
McGraw-Hill, 1960.
Your child will enjoy making up extra verses to this
absurd nursery rhyme.

Gretz, Susanna. *Teddy Bear's ABC.* Chicago: Follett,
1975.
Have fun making up sentences like those in the
book: "T is for tickling in a tent."

Hoberman, Mary Ann. *A House Is a House for Me.* Illus:
Betty Fraser. New York: Viking, 1978.
In this rhyme about houses of all kinds you and your
child will learn about houses you never even imag-
ined. It will be easy to make up new verses to this
rhyme and to make homemade houses, such as a
blanket draped over a card table.

Hopkins, Lee Bennett. *Go to Bed! A Book of Bedtime Poems*. Illus: Rosekrans Hoffman. New York: Alfred A. Knopf, 1979.

A picture book collection of poems depicting the pleasant and sometimes unpleasant aspects surrounding bedtime. Rosekrans Hoffman's fanciful drawings of impish creatures, whimsical pets, and tattered toys are dreamlike and entertaining. The book includes poems by Karla Kuskin, Robert Louis Stevenson, Charlotte Zolotow, and Joan Walsh Anglund.

Kessler, Ethel and Leonard. *All Aboard the Train*. Garden City, N.Y.: Doubleday, 1966.

This rhyming story tells the experiences of children on a train. Visit a railroad station after reading it to expand on the concepts presented.

———. *Big Red Bus*. Garden City, N.Y.: Doubleday, 1964.

Take a ride on a bus after reading this story. Listen to the noises and watch things go by.

Lear, Edward. *The Owl and the Pussy Cat and Other Nonsense*. Illus: Owen Wood. New York: Viking, 1978.

"The Owl and the Pussy Cat" and eight of Lear's most popular limericks are illustrated by Owen Wood. These detailed humorous, brightly colored illustrations are in an old-fashioned style.

McCord, David. *Every Time I Climb a Tree*. Illus: Marc Simont. Boston: Little, Brown, 1967.

A collection of poems about familiar places, things, and experiences such as trees and rocks. The anthology includes such favorite poems as "The Pickety Fence," "Pad and Pencil," and "This Is My Rock." This book might inspire you to create your own verses for common things.

Schmiderer, Dorothy. *The Alphabeast Book: An Abecedarium*. New York: Holt, Rinehart and Winston, 1971.

In a sequence of four frames for each letter of the alphabet, the letters are transformed into animals. In the first frame the letter is presented, in frames 2 and 3 it is reshaped until in frame 4 we see the animal. Your child might want to dramatize letter shapes by making them with her body. Or you might make your own alphabeast book.

Stevenson, Robert Louis. *A Child's Garden of Verses*. Illus: Brian Wildsmith. New York: Franklin Watts, 1966.

Many of the poems in this classic collection are about the everyday life of a child, for example, "My Shadow" and "The Swing." You'll have fun memorizing some poems to recite at appropriate times, such as while swinging, or when your child's shadow is sharp and noticeable.

Wildsmith, Brian. *Brian Wildsmith's ABC*. New York: Franklin Watts, 1963.

One simple picture represents each letter of the alphabet. The word is also given.

————. *Brian Wildsmith's Mother Goose*. New York: Franklin Watts, 1964.

If your child has been read nursery rhymes since infant days, you'll want a new collection for the pre-reading years. This one has some new rhymes and some familiar ones to be sung ("Hush-a-bye Baby," "Sing a Song of Sixpence," and "Bye, Baby Bunting"); chanted ("As I Was Going To St. Ives"); acted out ("Ride a Cock-horse"); and played with ("I Saw a Ship A-sailing" is fine for the bathtub).

Books for Science and Math Fun

Your prereader is rapidly expanding his concepts of the world. Curiosity, exploration, and thinking skills need encouragement during this time. You need books that get your child to ask questions and build a sense of wonder, in addition to those that encourage skills—counting, comparing and learning about the environment.

Aliki. *My Five Senses*. New York: Thomas Y. Crowell, 1972.

This book, which tells how we use our five senses, would be a good springboard to all sorts of activities around the house where we do use them: sorting laundry, smelling seasonings, listening to and identifying bird calls, learning different tastes, or playing "I spy with my little eyes"—the game where "it" gives one word describing an object (round, purple, fuzzy) and the others guess what it is.

Anno, Mitsumasa. *Anno's Counting Book*. New York: Thomas Y. Crowell, 1977.

Your child will enjoy counting the trees, fish, train cars, birds, buildings, and flowers in Anno's lovely, wordless color illustrations. Numbers from 1 to 12 are presented. You might want to count things in your own neighborhood.

Asimov, Isaac. *Animals of the Bible*. Illus: Howard Berelson. Garden City, N.Y.: Doubleday, 1978.

Animals of the Bible are illustrated in neutral colors. Short paragraphs tell about each animal and give the Biblical references to that animal. Some familiar animals are pictured (hippopotamus, leopard, goat, monkey), and some unusual animals are also shown, such as the fennec and the onager.

Barton, Bryon. *Wheels*. New York: Thomas Y. Crowell, 1979.

Find the wheels on many different vehicles. Discuss different kinds of wheels with your child—large wheels, small wheels, solid, spoked.

Bayley, Nicola. *One Old Oxford*. New York: Atheneum, 1977.

This book contains the illustration of an old English counting rhyme. The sentences contain tongue-twisting words that all begin with the same letter of the alphabet. As children get older they will have fun making up their own rhymes.

Baylor, Byrd. *Everybody Needs a Rock*. Illus: Peter Parnall. New York: Scribner's, 1974.

This book will inspire you to learn more about the desert and about rocks. Your child may enjoy talking about her own special places.

Burton, Virginia L. *The Little House*. Boston: Houghton Mifflin, 1942.

In this book, now in paperback, a little country house watches while the city grows up around it. The many types of transportation pictured might inspire you and your prereader to take some trips to see similar vehicles. A visit to a construction site will let you see the construction process at first hand.

Eastman, P. D. *What Time Is It?* New York: Random House, 1979.

A clock at the top of each page tells the time (hours only) for common daily activities. This is a small cardboard, spiral-bound book and can be opened flat to discuss the clocks.

Ets, Marie Hall. *Gilberto and the Wind*. New York: Viking, 1963.

Gilberto finds evidences of the wind and so will your child if you make a pinwheel or a kite, blow up a balloon, or make a toy sailboat.

Fisher, Aileen. *Going Barefoot*. Illus: Adrienne Adams. New York: Thomas Y. Crowell, 1960.

Footprints of many different animals point out the absurdity of animals wearing shoes—in rhyme. It would be great fun to search for footprints in the mud after reading this book. It's also appropriate for the child who is waiting not-so-patiently for warm weather so she can go barefoot.

Francoise, Chouchou. *Jeanne-Marie Counts Her Sheep*. New York: Scribner's, 1967.

A color and counting book your prereader will enjoy. Also available in paperback.

Gantos, Jack and Nicole Rubel. *The Perfect Pal*. Boston: Houghton Mifflin, 1979.

A child searches all over to find the perfect pal, especially in the pet store. You might take your child to a pet store after reading this book.

Hoban, Tana. *Count and See*. New York: Macmillan, 1972.

Black and white photographs of very common things that can be counted, such as bottle caps, eggs, and cookies. After reading the book, you and your child will be inspired to look all around you for things to count.

———. *Push, Pull, Empty, Full*. New York: Macmillan, 1972.

Another photographic book. This one illustrates concepts like push-pull, empty-full.

Hutchins, Pat. *Titch*. New York: Macmillan, 1971. Paperback edition, 1971.

Titch is small, but his contribution in planting a tiny seed is a big one. This is a good book to share at gardening time.

Krementz, Jill. *A Very Young Dancer*. New York: Alfred A. Knopf, 1977.

With high-quality photographs and a readable, narrative text, the reader follows a budding, young ballet dancer as she practices and participates in a professional New York production of the ballet, "The Nutcracker." If possible, you and your child might want to attend a local performance of the "Nutcracker" after reading this book.

Livermore, Elaine. *Three Little Kittens Lost Their Mittens*. Boston: Houghton Mifflin, 1979.

This book is really a visual perception game where the reader tries to find the lost mittens. Since visual perception is a prereading skill and since the pictures are appealing, a young child might enjoy the book.

Ungerer, Tomi. *Snail, Where Are You?* New York: Harper & Row, 1962.

Your child can find the elusive snail shape in pictures.

————. *Ask Me a Question*. New York: Harper & Row, 1968. Find the question mark shape in this one.

Zacharias, Thomas. *But Where is the Green Parrot?* Illus: Wanda Zacharias. New York: Delacorte Press, 1969.

See if you can find the parrot in each picture.

Cuddle Stories

Prereaders, who aren't hugged and cuddled as often as they were when they were infants and toddlers, relish quiet story times with their parents. Books that are best suited to these tender moments (often just before bedtime) are picture books that tell a story rather than books of information. Stories may be fantasies or may deal realistically with family life, everyday experiences, or the world outside the home. Scarier stories and stories that bring up disturbing situations might be shared early in the day rather than at bedtime.

Aardema, Verna. *Half-a-Ball-of-Kenki*. Illus: Diane Stanley Zuromskis. New York: Frederick Warne, 1979.
This Ashanti tale tells how the leopard got its spots. It might be compared with other "how" folktales.

Alexander, Martha. *Nobody Asked Me If I Wanted A Baby Sister*. New York: Dial Press, 1971. Paperback edition, 1977.
This would be an excellent little book to read after a new baby arrives in the household. In it a youngster tries to give his baby sister away until he is the only one who can get her to stop crying. Another way the story might be stretched is to provide a doll and doll-carriage for acting out the story.

Anglund, Joan Walsh. *Nibble, Nibble Mousekin: A Tale of Hansel and Gretel*. New York: Harcourt Brace, 1962. Paperback edition, 1977.
Read this one after your child has been lost and then found. You might make gingerbread or read *The Gingerbread Boy* afterwards. Lots of open-ended discussions present themselves as your child predicts, for example, what will happen to the witch's house.

Asch, Frank. *A Turtle Tale*. New York: Dial Press, 1978.
A turtle learns that the wise thing to do is to be flexible when the circumstances change.

Bemelmans, Ludwig. *Madeline*. New York: Viking, 1939. Paperback edition, 1977.
This is one of the perennially popular Madeline se-

ries, about an orphan's humorous encounters with the outside world.

Bernstein, Ruth Lercher. *I'll Draw a Meadow*. New York: Harper & Row, 1979.

Loneliness is the topic of this book. A young child asserts her desire to be alone—yet not too far from other people. A delicate book for quiet lap reading.

Breinburg, Petronella. *Shawn Goes to School*. Illus: Errol Lloyd. New York: Thomas Y. Crowell, 1974.

Shawn cries on the first day at nursery school, but discovers an understanding teacher, toys, and friends.

Bright, Robert. *Georgie*. Garden City, N.Y.: Doubleday, 1959.

Georgie the ghost appears in a series of humorous adventures. Halloween would be an appropriate time to share this book with your child. See if she can read the word "Georgie" in the text after you have pointed it out in the title.

Brown Marcia. *Once a Mouse*. New York: Scribner's, 1961.

The woodcut illustrations of this tale show a hermit's uses of magic. You can make prints with your prereader by making a simple design on a potato and cutting around it so that the print stands up above the rest of the potato. Dip it in tempera paint and make a design on paper.

Bulla, Clyde Robert. *Keep Running Allen!* Illus: Satomi Ichikawa. New York: Thomas Y. Crowell, 1978.

Allen, the youngest brother, always has to keep up with his older brothers and sister until the happiest day of his life when they join him on a hilltop to appreciate the soft grass and imagine figures in the clouds. Every child who is the youngest in the family will relate to Allen's troubles in keeping up with the big kids, and older children will enjoy learning about the perspective of younger ones. You might find it pleasant to sit in some soft grass and study the cloud formations with your child on a nice warm day.

Carle, Eric. *Pancakes, Pancakes*. New York: Pantheon, 1971. Paperback edition, 1975.

Jack's mother has him participate in every step of the procedure for making pancakes for breakfast. You won't be able to avoid having pancakes for breakfast after reading this. This book is also good for sequencing. Have your child tell you what happens first, next, and last.

———. *The Secret Birthday Message*. New York: Thomas Y. Crowell, 1972.

Young children love secrets, birthdays, messages, and puppies, which makes this book very likely to be a success. Try writing your prereader a short, simple secret message each morning on her chalkboard. After helping her read it, see if she can read it independently later in the day. For example, "Terry takes the garbage out today."

Carrick, Carol. *Paul's Christmas Birthday*. Illus: Donald Carrick. New York: Greenwillow, 1978.

For young children who are concerned that they will be cheated out of a proper birthday because their birthday falls too close to Christmas, this story has a solution. Santa comes twice.

Cohen, Miriam. *Will I Have A Friend?* Illus: Lillian Hoban. New York: Macmillan, 1967. Paperback edition, 1971.

To ease your child's anxiety about the first day at nursery school, this little book is a must.

Cressy, J. *Max the Mouse*. Illus: T. Cole. Englewood Cliffs, N.J.: Prentice-Hall, 1977.

Max does a turnabout by scaring a cat family. You might talk about fears with your child after reading this book.

Delaney, Ned. *Bert and Barney*. Boston: Houghton Mifflin, 1979.

Two best friends are masters at compromise until they have a big argument; but in the end they save each other. The illustrations add levity to a topic that for young children can be rather serious.

Duvoisin, Roger. *Petunia's Christmas*. New York: Alfred A. Knopf, 1952.

There are several "Petunia" books. In this one Petunia, a goose, comes up with some ingenious ways to save a gander from becoming a Christmas dinner. You and your child might try some problem-solving as you anticipate the outcome.

Ets, Marie Hall. *Play with Me*. New York: Viking, 1955.

At first the animals run away, but later they learn to be friends. You and your child might talk about animals or friends after reading this story.

Farber, Norma. *How Does It Feel to Be Old?* Illus: Trina Schart Hyman. New York: E. P. Dutton, 1979.

A sensitive rhymed story of all sorts of adventures with Grandma. On the last page both Grandma and grandchild speculate about the time when Grandma will die. A very perceptive, realistic handling of a topic many young children have questions about. The beautiful Grandma-grandchild relationship is one that most young children would relate to.

Gackenbach, Dick. *Harry and the Terrible Whatzit*. New York: Seabury, 1977.

Harry conquers his fear of the terrible whatzit in the cellar. Your child may be afraid of something very different from Harry's "whatzit," but the idea of overcoming any fear will strike a sympathetic chord.

———. *Claude and Pepper*. New York: Seabury, 1976.

Pepper the pup decides to leave home to explore the wide world. Claude helps Pepper realize how nice it is when someone loves you.

Grimm, Jacob L. *Snow White and the Seven Dwarfs*. Illus: Nancy Ekholm Berkert. New York: Farrar, Straus and Giroux, 1972.

In this traditional tale, good overcomes evil. You might compare this version with another one of the same tale, or try to act out the story.

Grimm, Jacob and Wilhelm. *The Shoemaker and the Elves*. Translated by W. Andrews. Illus: Adrienne Adams. New York: Scribner's, 1960.

The tiny elves who secretly help the shoemaker in the middle of the night reap the reward of new clothes. Your child might enjoy a visit to a shoe repair shop or factory after reading this story. Elves may also become a topic of conversation.

Hamilton, Morse and Emily. *My Name is Emily*. Illus: Jenni Oliver. New York: Greenwillow, 1979.

Emily returns from running away to find that her family loves her every bit as much as her new little baby sister. You might compare this story with *Peter's Chair*, by Keats.

Hoban, Russell. *Bedtime for Frances*. Illus: Garth Williams. New York: Harper & Row, 1960. Paperback edition, 1976.

There are many "Frances" books about the badger family and each relates to the everyday life of young children. Most children have tried the bedtime-delaying tactics used in this story.

Hughes, S. *Moving Molly*. Englewood Cliffs, N.J.: Prentice-Hall, 1978.

A family moves from a city to a house with a yard. Molly discovers new secret places and makes new friends. Read this book just before a move or just because Molly is an interesting girl to read about.

Hutchins, Pat. *One-Eyed Jake*. New York: Greenwillow, 1979.

A pirate who frightens his crew—the cook, the bo-sun, and the cabin boy—throws them out of the boat (and to safety) as the boat sinks under the weight of his stolen treasure. The illustrations and the absurdity of the situation make the pirate, who could be frightening to a young child, humorous. You might study some nautical terms along with this book.

Keats, Ezra Jack. *Peter's Chair*. New York: Harper & Row, 1967.

Peter feels a bit resentful that all of his belongings are being painted pink for the new baby—until he realizes that he is too big for his chair, and that this, too, should be painted. This would be a lovely book to share with a child whose mother is expecting a baby.

Kellogg, Steven. *Pinkerton, Behave!* New York: Dial Press, 1979.

All efforts to train Pinkerton, the dog, fail—until the day the robbers come. Any family who is trying to train a pet would enjoy this humorous book.

Kent, Jack. *Jack Kent's Hokus Pokus Bedtime Book*. New York: Random House, 1979.

The cartoon-like illustrations, the trademark of Jack Kent, accompany several tales: Aladdin, Toads and Diamonds, The Frog Prince, Jack and the Beanstalk, and The Golden Goose.

Krahn, Fernando. *The Family Minus*. New York: Parents' Magazine Press, 1977.

An ingenious mother of eight solves a problem when the car won't start.

Krasilovsky, Phyllis. *The Cow Who Fell in the Canal*. Illus: Peter Spier. Garden City, N.Y.: Doubleday, 1972.

Hendrika the cow falls into the canal, floats to the

cheese market on a raft, and surprises all the Dutch people. Lots of Dutch folkways are subtly presented in the illustrations and the text. You and your child might want to visit a cheese factory or learn more about Holland after reading this book.

Krauss, Robert. *Milton the Early Riser*. Illus: José and Adrienne Aruego. New York: E. P. Dutton, 1972, Paperback edition, 1974.

In this very short, simple story Milton, a panda, arises before anyone else does. By the time the others awake, he is fast asleep again. Good for a child who is an early riser.

Kroll, Steven, *Is Milton Missing?* Illus: Dick Gackenbach. New York: Holiday, 1975.

Finding a lost dog is the adventure in this tale, but you needn't have lost something to enjoy this good story.

Lapp, Eleanor J. *In the Morning Mist*. Illus: David Cunningham. Chicago: Albert Whitman, 1978.

A boy and his grandfather go fishing very early in the morning. You will enjoy this short, simple story.

Lindgren, Astrid. *Christmas in the Stable*. Illus: H. Wiberg. New York: Coward-McCann, 1962.

This story of the first Christmas will help set the mood for the Christmas season. It is set in Sweden, and you and your child may want to learn more about Christmas customs in other lands after reading it.

———. *The Tomten*. Illus: H. Wiberg. New Jersey: Coward-McCann, 1961.

A tale of elves in a farm in winter. It would be good to read this book in conjunction with a visit to a farm. You might also want to compare this with other stories about elves.

Lionni, Leo. *In the Rabbitgarden*. New York: Pantheon, 1975.

In this parallel to Adam and Eve, the serpent saves the day.

Lloyd, Errol. *Nini at the Carnival*. New York: Thomas Y. Crowell, 1978.

A fairy godmother solves Nini's problem of having no costume by making her queen of the carnival. This book might be nice to share with a child who is self-conscious about not having a Halloween costume—or just about being "different."

Lobel, Arnold. *A Treeful of Pigs*. Illus: Anita Lobel. New York: Greenwillow, 1979.

A farmer who promises to care for some pigs does not, until the humorous situation demands that he relieve his overburdened wife. You might relate this book to family responsibilities or visit a pig farm to stretch this book with your child.

McCloskey, Robert. *Blueberries for Sal*. New York: Viking, 1948. Paperback edition, 1976.

Sal and her mother encounter a young bear and its mother while picking blueberries on Blueberry Hill. Most young children like to gather things in pails, as Sal does in the book. If you can, accompany this story by a berry picking expedition with your child.

———. *Make Way for Ducklings*. New York: Viking, 1941. Paperback edition, 1976.

A mother duck settles upon the Boston Common as a suitable place to raise her ducklings. This book is a good one to read just after feeding the ducks at a local pond.

———. *One Morning in Maine*. New York: Viking, 1952.

Sal is older in this story than when she picked blueberries. She has a little sister Jane. Sal loses her first tooth in the mud while clamming with her father, then gets her secret wish of a chocolate ice cream cone. This delightful book shows a very supportive father, and is a good one to read when your child discovers the first loose baby tooth. Also, the sea scenes, with a loon, gulls, and a seal, make it an ideal book for a beach visit.

McPhail, David. *Grandfather's Cake*. New York: Scribner's, 1979.

Andrew and Peter and Peaches, their pony, encounter a number of trials in the woods before safely reaching their grandfather with a piece of chocolate cake. The enemies (a fox, a bear, and a robber) can be frightening, but the warmth of the story about a grandmother baking a chocolate cake, and the children delivering it in spite of their temptation to eat it on the way, overcomes any real fear. Lovely black and white sketches illustrate the story.

Maestro, Betsy. *Harriet Goes to the Circus*. Illus: Giulio Maestro. New York: Crown, 1977.

Harriet is first in the line of animals waiting to see the circus, but when the door opens, she goes from first to last. Since waiting in line is central to school and life experiences, the book is a good one to share with your prereader.

Mahy, Margaret. *The Boy Who Was Followed Home*. Illus: Steven Kellogg. New York: Franklin Watts, 1975.

Hippos follow Robert home. This story is a good example of problem-solving.

Mayer, Mercer. *There's a Nightmare in My Closet*. New York: Dial Press, 1968.

The nightmare turns out to be more frightened than the boy in the story, who graciously lets him share his bed and tucks him in. Fears of the dark can be discussed after meeting this frightened nightmare.

Preston, Edna M. *One Dark Night*. Illus: Kurt Werth. New York: Viking, 1969.

Halloween trick-or-treaters are scared by a mouse.

Raskin, Ellen. *Spectacles*. New York: Atheneum, 1968. Paperback edition, 1972.

Spectacles really aren't so bad after all if they help you see things more clearly. Your child might enjoy reading this with a set of play glasses or sunglasses. You might talk about things you see to learn more about your sense of sight. A child who has just gotten eyeglasses and is not comfortable with them would enjoy this book.

Rey, Hans A. *Curious George*. Boston: Houghton Mifflin, 1941.

There is a long series of books about Curious George, a monkey who gets into mischief. Although the illustrations are less than works of art, George is a very popular fellow. The trouble George gets into is the kind children themselves get into, and George also expresses some common fears children have. Most of the books are also available in paperback.

Sharmat, Marjorie Weinman. *The Trolls of 12th Street*. Illus: Ben Shecter. New York: Coward, McCann and Geoghegan, 1979.

Trolls are popular these days. These personable little ones beg to see the world outside their cave until they are finally allowed to do so. You might talk about limits and what is beyond the limits of your child's world.

Seidler, Rosalie. *Panda Cake*. New York: Parent's Magazine Press, 1978.

Willie and his little brothers shop for the ingredients to bake a cake—and the cake-baking experience turns out to be a humorous one. Shop with your child, then bake a cake.

Spier, Peter. *Noah's Ark*. Garden City, New York: Doubleday, 1977.

Detailed color pictures of the Bible story are ideal for storytelling and talking about the animals.

Steig, William. *Tiffky Doofky*. New York: Farrar, Straus and Giroux, 1978.

Early childhood educators claim that preschoolers love slapstick humor. If that is the case, your child will enjoy watching a dog garbage collector find his love.

Stone, Elberta. *I'm Glad I'm Me*. Illus: Margaret Wise Brown. New Jersey: G. P. Putnam, 1971.

A city child pretends to be lots of things, but most of all he likes being himself.

Tompert, Ann. *Little Fox Goes to the End of the World*. Illus: John Wallner. New York: Crown, 1976.

Little Fox plans her trip in the wild world and her Mother encourages her imagination, but says she'll be glad to see her when she gets home.

Turkle, Brinton. *Rachel and Obadiah*. New York: E. P. Dutton, 1978.

Similar to *Thy Friend, Obadiah* and *Obadiah the Bold*, this sequel about the Quaker family is thoroughly charming. Rachel, the younger sister, wins out over her older brother who is showing off, yet still shares her treasure in the end. This is an excellent book for siblings to share. The sea scenes make the book a nice companion for a trip to a harbor.

Waber, Bernard. *Ira Sleeps Over*. Boston: Houghton Mifflin, 1972.

A little boy can't decide whether to take his teddy bear next door to Reggie's house for an overnight visit. This would be an interesting book to share before a night when your child is sleeping at someone's house. Or, you might talk about the child's prized possessions.

Williamson, Jane. *The Trouble with Alaric*. New York: Farrar, Straus and Giroux, 1975.

A dog acts like a person, but finds he can't cope with

the responsibilities. As your child gradually assumes responsibilities, share this book with him.

Yaffe, Alan. *The Magic Meatballs*. Illus: Karen Born Anderson. New York: Dial Press, 1979.

When Marvin has trouble being heard in his family he changes them all into meats and then back again into humans. Young children love to feel that they have some measure of power over adults. Read this when power battles are in full swing.

Zalban, Jane. *Lyle and Humus*. New York: Macmillan, 1974.

A monkey and an elephant are circus friends. Their friendship is put to the test, but all ends well. Read this story when your child is developing and testing friendships.

Zemach, Kaethe. *The Beautiful Rat*. New York: Four Winds Press, 1979.

Yoshiko's parents finally accept the fact that she will marry a rat, after the sun, the cloud, the wind, and the stone wall prove unworthy of her affections. This silly tale could inspire imaginative thinking on the part of young children.

Zolotow, Charlotte. *William's Doll*. New York: Harper & Row, 1972.

In this story William wants and gets a doll. It is a warm story to be read while cuddling a favorite doll and breaks down the stereotype that says a boy can't play with dolls.

———. *If It Weren't For You*. Illus: Ben Shecter. New York: Harper & Row, 1966.

This book is about sibling rivalry. It would be appropriate to discuss feelings about siblings, and plan joint projects like carving a pumpkin or baking a cake together.

Puppet and Flannelboard Stories

Children who are prereaders gain confidence as storytellers when they have props to stimulate their storytelling. A flannelboard and puppet theatre are two easily designed props that will get abundant use, not only from your child, but probably the neighborhood children as well.

You can make your flannelboard by stapling flannel or felt to plywood or heavy cardboard. A portable board might include hinges and handles. Story characters are easily traced onto pellon fabric and cut out. Slightly more sturdy and colorful characters can be made by tracing storybook pictures onto oaktag cardboard with carbon paper. Color with permanent color magic markers. Cut out and glue strips of sandpaper on the backs and your characters will stick to the flannel. Store the pieces for each story in a separate envelope.

Appliance boxes convert rather easily into puppet theaters. Fancier models are made out of wood and have curtains from scraps of cloth. If these more finished products are unavailable, a box turned on its side will do. Simple puppets can be made from socks, gloves, or mittens decorated with scraps, buttons and yarn. Stick puppets can be made from construction paper pasted onto popsicle sticks, tongue depressers, or dowels. More sophisticated, long-lasting puppets are easily made from paper mâché. Store your puppets in shoeboxes on shelves inside your theatre.

Stories that are good for dramatization have few characters, few changes of scene, lots of action, and simple, often repetitive, language. The following tales have phonograph records accompanying them.

Asbjornsen, P. C. *The Three Billy Goats Gruff.* Illus: Marcia Brown. New York: Harcourt Brace, 1957.

Good triumphs over evil as each succeeding billy goat outwits the great ugly troll.

Galdone, Paul. *Gingerbread Boy*. New York: Seabury, 1975.

Make gingerbread cookies to munch while reading or telling this story.

————. *Three Billy Goats Gruff*. New York: Seabury, 1973.

Another version of the favorite tale. Your child will soon be able to tell this story independently on a flannelboard.

————. *The Three Little Pigs*. New York: Seabury, 1970.

In addition to retelling this story either with puppets or flannelboard figures, your child might like to taste turnips and help churn butter.

Harper, Wilhelmina. *The Gunniwolf*. Illus: William Wiesner. New York: G. P. Dutton, 1967.

Your child will join in the singing as the girl in the forest escapes the Gunniwolf. This story is fun to act out, also.

McGovern, Ann. *Too Much Noise*. Boston: Houghton Mifflin, 1967. Paperback, New York: Scholastic Book Services, 1980.

Books with Few or No Words

Another stimulus for storytelling is a book with no words or very few, which can be "read" by prereaders because it has pictures that tell the story. Preschoolers "reading" these books can then retell the stories orally or dictate a version to be written. Wordless picture books can thus nurture a love of books, stimulate creative language expression, extend critical thinking skills, and develop a sense of reading before children have been formally taught how to read.

When using a wordless book for the first time, it is helpful to encourage your child to look at the entire book before attempting to tell the story. Then he can go back and "read" it. You can ask questions which will encourage your child to give an interpretation of the story at the appropriate time ("How would you tell this story?" "What is happening in these pictures?" "How do you think the girl feels? Why?") Having your child pretend to be one of the characters and tell the story from that person's point of view may stimulate her thinking, too.

Other activities your child might enjoy would be making a tape-recorded soundtrack for the story to be played as someone looks at the book; thinking of further adventures of the main character; or dramatizing a scene from the book.

De Paola, Tomie. *Pancakes for Breakfast*. New York: Harcourt Brace Jovanovich, 1978.
> A little old lady's attempts to have pancakes for breakfast are hindered by a scarcity of supplies and the havoc created by her pets. She finally smells pancakes at her neighbors' house and eats breakfast with them. You won't be able to resist making pancakes after reading this story.

Krahn, Fernando. *How Santa Claus Had a Long and Difficult Journey Delivering His Presents*. New York: Delacorte Press, 1970. Paperback edition, 1977.
> Santa is getting ready to deliver his presents. Tragedy strikes when the reins break and the reindeer fly away, leaving Santa and the bag of toys on the ground. The toys try to pull the sleigh but can't. Angels rescue Santa by flying him to his reindeer.

Mayer, Mercer. *A Boy, a Frog, and a Dog; A Boy, a Frog, a Dog and a Friend; Frog Goes to Dinner*. New

York: Dial Press, 1974. Paperback edition, New York: Scholastic Book Services, 1980.

Turkle, Brinton. *Deep in the Forest*. New York: E. P. Dutton, 1976.

A wordless picture book which tells the traditional story of "Goldilocks and the Three Bears" but with a new twist—a baby bear wreaks havoc in a pioneer cabin. Every child loves seeing this kind of chaos. The book has soft, gentle illustrations.

Schermer, Judith. *Mouse in House*. Boston: Houghton Mifflin, 1979.

A wordless book illustrated in gay-nineties style shows a family that nearly tears their house apart trying to oust a mouse. Their daughter saves the day with an inventive scheme for removing the mouse. Your child might like to read other mice stories along with this one.

Notes

[1] May Hill Arbuthnot. *Reading in the Home* (Glenview, Illinois: Scott, Foresman, 1969) p. 21.

[2] Nancy Larrick. *A Parent's Guide to Children's Reading* (New York: Bantam Books, 1975) 24–26.

[3] American Library Association. *Let's Read Together: Books for Family Enjoyment* (Chicago: American Library Association, 1969) p. x.

References

American Library Association. *Let's Read Together: Books for Family Enjoyment*. Chicago: American Library Association, 1969.

American Library Association. *Notable Children's Books 1940–1970*. Chicago: American Library Association, 1977.

Arbuthnot, May Hill. *Children and Books*. Chicago: Scott, Foresman, 1977.

Cianciolo, Patricia Jean, ed. *Picture Books for Children*. Chicago: American Library Association, 1973.

Coody, Betty. *Using Literature with Young Children*. Dubuque, Iowa: William C. Brown, 1973.

Huck, Charlotte S. *Children's Literature in the Elementary School*, 3rd ed. New York: Holt, Rinehart and Winston, 1976.

Larrick, Nancy. *A Parent's Guide to Children's Reading*, 4th Revision. Garden City, N.Y.: Doubleday, 1975. Bantam Paperback edition, 1975.

Sutherland, Zena, and May Hill Arbuthnot. *Children and Books*, 5th ed. Glenview, Ill.: Scott, Foresman, 1977.

IV

Sharing Literature with Your Beginning Reader

WHITE SHEEP, WHITE SHEEP
ON A BLUE HILL.

    "I'm reading it! I'm reading it!"

WHEN THE WIND STOPS
YOU STAND STILL.[1]

    "I read it all!" (sigh) "I really did!!!"

Very little can surpass the exuberance of a child who just realizes that he has read an entire passage by himself! It is a time of celebration. The praise and attention this feat earns will encourage future performances as well as help to establish a personal enjoyment of literature. Learning to read, however, is only one step toward making a habit of reading for pleasure. Other factors that will enrich and reinforce the child's first independent reading accomplishments are: an exposure to many different types of books; the presence of reading models; the opportunity for independent experiences in the library (choosing books, checking them out himself), your continuing to read aloud to your child; and an active involvement with literature that extends beyond just reading the printed word. Specific activities, which can be carried out at home, will enhance the value of reading literature. Before starting such activities, it is important that you become familiar with some of the characteristics of appropriate literature for the young reader.

Literature for the Beginning Reader

As your child begins to read, he will most likely want to revisit old favorites that were previously read aloud to him—familiar folk and fairy tales, and stories he particularly liked. Some of these "old friends" will be too difficult for the child to read independently since many picture storybooks are on a third grade reading level or higher. However, even though your child cannot sound out or sight read each printed word, she will still be able to follow a familiar story and will often fill in her own words for those she cannot read.

It is not unusual to overhear a parent at a public library say, when his child insists on checking out a book that has been read and reread at home: "We've had that book before. Why not choose a different one?" "Besides," the parent might add, "It's too hard for you to read by yourself." Comments like these may lead to loud protests, or even a tantrum, reflecting the child's genuine disappointment that her old friend Curious George, The Cat in the Hat, or whoever, must be left behind. This need not happen. If your child has favorite books he likes to read, let him. This continued exposure to written material above his reading level in familiar books whose stories he knows so well, can be an important learning experience.

Another way of dealing with a book that is too hard for your child to read alone is to "team-read" it. Do this by holding the book so that you both can see the words. Then read the book together, encouraging the child to read the words as you do. If you come to a word the child doesn't know, continue reading and she will join in when she can. This read-along or imitative method will help give the child a sense of story, as well as practice in phrasing groups of words and a feeling of accomplishment in reading. Another way to team-read is for you to look at a page and lightly underline the words the child recognizes. Do the same with repetitive phrases, names, and places, which children usually learn to read quickly. Then read the page together with you filling in the unknown words. If you do this with an entire book, it should not be long before your child will be reading it privately on her own.

Several positive things take place when you team read. Your child will very likely increase his reading sight-vocabulary, which means that he will recognize more words instantly. By reading in a familiar context your child might use the known words in the story as clues to unknown ones. Hence, she can practice several reading skills independently in a pleasurable, non-frustrating atmosphere. Your child will also be learning in the presence of familiar "friends," his favorite book characters.

By reading books that are above her level, the beginning reader gets practice in developing a sense of story.

Early readers often just "call" words, ignoring the over-all meaning or message of the story. Team reading and discussion of the book after it is read will help your child realize that the words he recognizes work together to give meaning to the story.

You might want to encourage your child to borrow one familiar book on each library visit, on the condition that she also select some that are new to her. In order to help the child select books that he can read, we encourage you to browse through as many books as possible so that you may become familiar with the variety available for selection. If your child is just beginning to recognize printed words and phrases, you will want to watch for the following features as you help her select books for independent silent reading.

1. *The amount of print on each page.*

Try to determine if your child will be comfortable with the number of words and sentences on each page. One or two sentences are about as much as the beginning reader can handle. As you observe your child's interaction with reading materials, try to note how much of each page she can absorb independently without becoming frustrated. A book with such a limited amount of print is sometimes labeled "Beginning To Read," "Early I Can Read," or "Read-Alone." Two examples are *The Day I Had To Play With My Sister*[2] and *The Big Hello*.[3] Sentences such as "I will find you," and "What are you crying about?" are representative of the ones your child will encounter.

2. *The clarity and number of illustrations.*

The adage "A picture is worth a thousand words" is particularly true for the beginning reader. As you select books, note whether the illustrations help the reader understand the printed message and especially any new, long words. Be certain that the objects in the illustrations are clearly presented and easy to define. Many books available for the young child are cluttered. Busy pages may help the preschooler extend his vocabulary and knowledge of concepts, but when your child begins to read on his own, the book's pages should be simple and uncluttered. *Titch* [4] is an example of a simple, uncluttered book. The word *bicycle* may not be familiar, but the page is so designed that the reader will automatically focus his attention on the bicycle in the illustration. There is a great deal of white space. The young reader can readily pick out the words to be read and the meaning is reinforced by a clear, easily distinguished illustration.

3. *Repetition of words and phrases.*

Nothing reinforces a beginning reader more positively than repeatedly meeting instantly recognized words in a book. *The Teeny Tiny Woman* [5] and *Too Much Noise* [6] are examples of books with such repetition. In *The Teeny Tiny Woman*, the phrase "teeny tiny" is often repeated several times in a sentence. If your child cannot read all the words, read the book together. Slide your hand under the words as you read them, and as your child follows along he could read "teeny tiny" each time is occurs. You might try to read such a story over and over, speaking more quickly with each successive reading. In *Too Much Noise*, an elderly man visits the wise man of the village to complain about all the noises in the house—the squeaking of the bed and the whistling of the tea kettle—that bother him. In each of a series of meetings, the wise man tells the elderly man to take a different animal into his house. Each animal adds a sound to those that already annoy the man. Finally, the wise man advises that all the animals be removed, and the householder finds that the original sounds were not as bothersome as he thought. Throughout the book sound effects and phrases are repeated. Such repetition helps the reader anticipate the next episode in the story and successfully read phrases and sentences that occur often.

It sometimes seems to be more than a parent can take to have to read one book over and over and over again, especially one with much repetition. Remember, however, that during the beginning stages of reading independence, it is comforting to the child to meet familiar words and phrases many times during a story.

In addition, you could try the "two finger test" as one way to see how successfully your child is able to read a given book. To do this test select a page near the middle of the book. Ask her to read all the words on the page that she knows. If at least *two* words are not recognized by sight, the page, and most likely the book, will be too hard for independent reading just now. This does not mean that you shouldn't bring home the book. It does mean that it will have to be read aloud to the child, or team-read. Children at this beginning stage can be taught to use the two finger test as one way to select books they can read.

It is important to identify many different types of books that your child can read. During the early stages of reading independence many are under the impression that all that children can read independently is "Oh, Jane" and "Look, Dick." This is not true. There are many children's books of fiction and non-fiction, picture/concept books, and poetry appropriate for the beginning reader. The books labeled "I Can Read," "Read-Alone," "Early Ready To Read" or something similar are those that have been designed especially for the beginning reader. Many libraries have separate sections that contain books of this kind only. At one time such books were considered bland and were rather like beginning reading texts used in schools. However, many of the newer early reading books available in libraries and bookstores have well-developed story lines, well-drawn illustrations, and more sophisticated formats. These books cover a variety of subjects and interests. It is important that you become familiar with the material in a series like "I Can Read Science," "I Can Read History," and "I Can Read Sports." The information presented is clear and worthwhile. Adults have commented that they have learned things about animals, historic events, or other subjects that they never knew before. Many biographies of people familiar to children are also available in simple formats for the young reader.

It is important to remember that there are many different areas of literature and that more than just general fiction is available to the beginning reader. We suggest that you become acquainted with your local children's librarian. She or he will be delighted to point out the sections of the library set aside for beginning readers and to show you the specific books they would recommend from their experiences of working with beginning readers. Bookstore personnel can also be very helpful to parents who want to know more about books for their beginners. Tell the bookstore manager the types and levels of reading material you are looking for. You may in this way encourage the bookseller to order more of those kinds of books.

Helping Your Child Become an Independent Reader

As your child begins to spend more concentrated time looking at a page, or starts to read selected words or sentences on a page, he is probably ready to attempt to read a whole page or even a short book alone. A child of our acquaintance liked to imitate her mother reading; she read through a number of paperback picture books with a limited amount of print in this way. One day the child told her mother that she had read a book "all by herself." To her surprise and her daughter's pleasure, the mother found that it was a book new to the child, not one they had read together. From that point on, the daughter read independently, as well as continuing to "read" more difficult books with her mother.

There are a variety of ways you can encourage your child to become an independent reader. Be certain to plan for a period of the day which you both know as a time for reading aloud together. Turn all radios and television sets off. Focusing absolute attention on your child at this time is one important indication that you value both reading and your child. And the child seems to experience an "ego triumph" when he can share a book aloud with you.

As your child reads to you, be generous with praise. Offer compliments. "My goodness, you really sounded like the Little Red Hen!" Such comments will reinforce the growth your child is making in school in oral phrasing, pauses for punctuation, and conversational or character voice tones. When you read aloud to the child, your intonations serve as her model. In one family, the father always adds dimension to the characters in books by giving different voices to each character. As his son then reads aloud to him, the boy assigns similar vocal tones to the different characters.

On occasion your child will become frustrated when trying to read a book aloud. When this happens, you might try team reading, so that the child is still reading to you but is not put on the spot or "frozen" by words she does not know; she can skip them since they will be read by you. This is one way to expose your child to unknown words as well as to increase the fluency of her oral reading.[7]

As your child becomes successful with books that have an increasing amount of print on a page, you might take turns reading alternate pages. Sometimes, when a child completes a page in a book, it is a pleasure and possibly a relief to hear you read the next one. Remember that for the beginning reader, reading, although enjoyable, can also be hard work! Before using this strategy, be certain your child actually can read an entire page. You will want him to be successful. Approach it gradually; begin by taking "sentence turns" and then, "paragraph turns." Once a book has been mastered—once your child can read it fluently—then encourage him to read it many times. Have your child read it to your next door neighbor, to a younger child, to a friend, to a teacher. Tape-record the story and mail it to grandparents or other relatives. The positive reception of such a tape will enhance your child's self-concept as a reader as well as provide a sort of drill for mastering the words and phrases of the story.

To help your child comprehend the material to the greatest degree possible, you might look together at all the illustrations in the entire book before reading the first word. After the illustrations have been examined, guess together what might happen in the story. Your child will be interested to see if your predictions are similar to hers. Prediction prior to reading will help your child begin to think about the content of the story. It will also encourage active thinking while reading, because she will be checking to see if the predictions were right. After the story is read, you and your child might chat about the story and the illustrations and see how well you both guessed what would happen. During this chat, you might also comment about the characters. Statements like "Petunia was really surprised when she found out the book had pages!" may encourage a response from your child. This is one way to show that the content of books can make for interesting conversation. It also reinforces the idea that you are really interested in what the child's book is about.

Although this is the time in your child's learning development that he is beginning to read books independently, it is an especially important time for you to read aloud to him regularly. As we've said, many of the books about subjects in which your child might be interested are written at a reading level too difficult for a beginning reader. By reading aloud you continue to stretch the child's interest and attention span, and develop his listening vocabulary. By selecting books on a variety of topics you also can expand his conceptual ideas in many areas.

We suggest that you set aside a specific time each day or evening to read a "Sustaining Book" to your child. (A "Sustaining Book" was Winnie the Pooh's only sustenance after he ate too much honey and got stuck in the entrance to Rabbit's hole, until dieting slimmed him down enough to get out.)

> "I'm afraid no meals," said Christopher Robin, "because of getting thin quicker. But we *will* read to you."

> Bear began to sigh, and then found he couldn't because he was so tight stuck; and a tear rolled down his eye, as he said:

> "Then would you read a Sustaining Book, such as would help and comfort a Wedged Bear in Great Tightness?"

So for a week Christopher Robin read that sort of book at the North end of Pooh . . .[8]

"That sort of book" is one that will take several reading sessions to complete. This is a time to read material that the child can follow and understand, and that is longer or more difficult than she could read independently. This is also a time to read books that will let the imagination travel to new places and to meet characters who have adventures that can be vicariously enjoyed. You might encourage your child to make a bookmark for the "Sustaining Book" you are reading.

A suggested list follows of "Sustaining Books" that have been well received by young readers. We encourage you to select books on topics which interest you as well, because your feeling for the book's contents, positive or negative, will be conveyed as you read aloud. One idea is to read the first in a series. As your child becomes a more competent reader, he might well want to continue on his own with succeeding books in the series because of having been introduced to them during the reading aloud time. The limited list below is merely to give you an idea of the types of books that are appropriate.

Suggested "Sustaining Books" for Reading Aloud

Asbjørnsen, Peter Christian. *East of the Sun and West of the Moon*. Translated by George W. Dasent. Illus: Edgar and Ingri d'Aulaire. New York: Macmillan, 1953.

Atwater, Richard and Florence. *Mr. Popper's Penguins*. Illus: Robert Lawson. Boston: Little, Brown, 1938.

Bond, Michael. *A Bear Called Paddington*. (series) Boston: Houghton Mifflin, 1960.

Bulla, Clyde. *The Sword in the Tree*. Illus: Paul Galdone. New York: Thomas Y. Crowell, 1956.

Caudill, Rebecca. *Did You Carry the Flag Today, Charley?* New York: Holt, Rinehart and Winston, 1964.

Cleary, Beverly. *Ramona and her Father*. (series) New York: William Morrow, 1977.

Dalgliesh, Alice. *The Bears on Hemlock Mountain*. Illus: Helen Sewell. New York: Scribner's, 1952.

Estes, Eleanor. *The Moffats*. (series) Illus: Louis Slobodkin. New York: Harcourt Brace, 1941.

Hale, Lucretia. *The Complete Peterkin Papers*. Boston: Houghton Mifflin, 1960.

Hodges, Margaret. *The Wave*. Illus: Blair Lent. Boston: Houghton Mifflin, 1964.

Kipling, Rudyard. *Just-So Stories*. Illus: Etienne Delessert. Garden City, N.Y.: Doubleday, 1972.

Milne, A. A. *Winnie-The-Pooh*. (series) Illus: Ernest H. Shepard. New York: E. P. Dutton, 1926.

Ness, Evaline. *Sam, Bangs, and Moonshine*. New York: Holt, Rinehart and Winston, 1966.

Travers, Pamela. *Mary Poppins*. (series) Illus: Mary Shepard. New York: Harcourt Brace, 1934.

Untermeyer, Louis, ed. *Aesop's Fables*. Illus: Alice and Martin Provensen. London: Golden Press, 1965.

White, E. B. *Stuart Little*. New York: Harper & Row, 1945.

Williams, Jay. *The Practical Princess*. Illus: Friso Henstra. New York: Parents' Magazine Press, 1969.

At other times you will want to read a picture book in one sitting. We also encourage you to read aloud non-fiction books and poetry. You might alternate reading fiction and non-fiction. A poem could become part of your daily reading together. The poem could be one that fits in with the theme of the longer book you are reading or is a familiar favorite, or a well-known one that you want your child to hear or that has verses relating to events and objects in your child's own life.

A bibliography of suggested non-fiction books to read aloud and a bibliography of suggested poetry anthologies and collections is listed here for your reference. It must be stressed that both bibliographies are only samples of the literature available for children and are not to be considered an inclusive list.

Suggested Non-fiction Books for Reading Aloud

Adler, David A. *Redwoods Are the Tallest Trees in the World*. New York: Thomas Y. Crowell, 1978.

Baylor, Byrd. *Before You Came This Way*. New York: E. P. Dutton, 1969.

Borton, Helen. *A Picture Has A Special Look*. New York: Abelard-Schuman, 1961.

Carrick, Carol. *Beach Bird*. New York: Dial Press, 1973.

Klein, Norma. *Girls Can Be Anything*. New York: E. P. Dutton, 1973.

Lobel, Arnold. *On The Day Peter Stuyvesant Sailed Into Town*. New York: Harper & Row, 1971.

Milgrom, Harry. *Adventures With A Paper Cup*. New York: E. P. Dutton, 1968.

Parnall, Peter. *A Dog's Book of Birds*. New York: Scribner's, 1977.

Ruben, Patricia. *True or False?* Philadelphia: Lippincott, 1978. (A family participation/discussion book)

Sasek, Miroslav. *This is New York*. (series) New York: Macmillan, 1960.

Selsam, Millicent. *A First Look At The World of Plants*. New York: Walker, 1978.

Showers, Paul. *What Happens to a Hamburger?* New York: Thomas Y. Crowell, 1970.

Tresselt, Alvin. *The Beaver Pond*. New York: Lothrop, Lee & Shepard, 1970.

Weiss, Harvey. *What Holds It Together?* Boston: Little, Brown, 1977.

Wyler, Rose and Gerald Ames. *Secrets In Stones*. New York: Four Winds Press, 1971.

Suggested Poetry Anthologies and Single-Poet Collections

Aldis, Dorothy. *All Together: A Child's Treasury of Verse*. New York: G. P. Putnam, 1952.

Arbuthnot, May Hill and Shelton L. Root, Jr., eds. *Time For Poetry*, 3rd ed. Glenview, Ill.: Scott, Foresman, 1968.

Clifton, Lucille. *Some of the Days of Everett Anderson*. New York: Holt, Rhinehart and Winston, 1970.

Cole, William. *The Birds and Beasts Were There*. New York: World, 1963.

de Paola, Tomie. *Songs of the Fog Maiden*. New York: Holiday House, 1979.

Ferris, Helen, ed. *Favorite Poems Old and New*. Garden City, N.Y.: Doubleday, 1957.

Fisher, Aileen. *Feathered Ones and Furry*. Illus. Eric Carle. New York: Thomas Y. Crowell, 1970.

————. *I Stood Upon A Mountain*. New York: Thomas Y. Crowell, 1979.

Fujikawa, Guy, ed. *A Child's Book of Poems*. New York: Grosset and Dunlap, 1969.

Hopkins, Lee Bennett. *Me! A Book of Poems*. New York: Seabury, 1970.

Kroll, Steven. *Sleepy Ida and Other Nonsense Poems*. New York: Pantheon, 1977.

Kuskin, Karla. *Any Me I Want To Be*. New York: Harper & Row, 1972.

Lewis, Richard. *In A Spring Garden*. New York: Dial Press, 1965.

Livingstone, Myra Cohn. *Whispers and Other Poems*. New York: Harcourt Brace, 1959.

McCord, David. *One At A Time; His Collected Poems For The Young*. Boston: Little, Brown, 1977.

Merriam, Eve. *Catch A Little Rhyme*. New York: Atheneum, 1966.

Richards, Laura. *Tirra, Lirra; Rhymes Old and New*. Boston: Little, Brown, 1955.

Starbird, Kaye. *Don't Ever Cross A Crocodile*. Philadelphia: Lippincott, 1963.

Trip, Wallace. *A Great Big Ugly Man Came Up and Tied His Horse To Me, A Book of Nonsense Verse*. Boston: Little, Brown, 1973.

Untermeyer, Louis, ed. *The Golden Treasury of Poetry*. New York: Golden Press, 1959.

Providing a Stimulating Home Reading Environment

"Books, books, everywhere! Which one shall I read?" If there is an obvious abundance of any kind of thing in a household, it is usually an indication that these are things of value to that household. This is certainly true of books and among the multitude should be books appropriate to each member of the family.

It has been our experience that many adults require that their child read some time in the course of each day. However, in many of these same families the child reads alone. The parent often is "too busy" or perhaps out of the habit of reading. If there is a regularly designated time when the adults and older siblings are seen reading, it is a helpful example of the importance and enjoyment of reading.

We definitely encourage borrowing books from your local schools and libraries. However, books take on a more personal meaning if one is able to own a few favorites or perhaps anticipate a book as a gift for a birthday or other holiday. Each child should have a shelf, drawer, bookbox, or a bookcase where he can house those special books of his own as well as those books that have been borrowed.

The presence of children's periodicals, such as *Cricket Magazine*[9] and *National Geographic World*,[10] intermingled on the coffee table or other places in the home with magazines read by adults is another indication that reading is valued. It also is one way to provide for a variety of types of reading materials. To demonstrate to the child that the magazines contain material of interest, parents should browse through them (preferably while the child is watching) and read an article or feature. Both of the magazines named above contain articles that can be enjoyed by the parent as well as the child. *National Geographic World* often has visual puzzles that intrigue the beginning reader and help to sharpen her visual acuity.

Developing Family Reading Habits

In our multi-media world, there are many choices for recreational or leisure time activity. Some take less effort than others. It must be the adults of the home who set the requirements for such choices. Reading is a recreational activity. Parents are responsible for seeing that appropriate books are available for children to read, and that there is a specific place and time for reading.

One family has a nightly "read-in" as soon as the kitchen is in order after the evening meal. They find that this activity brings everyone together at least once a day during the week and, when possible, on weekends. There are three adults in the family, two parents and a grandmother, and four children, aged 4, 7, 10, and 13. Each reads to himself or herself. The two older children are capable readers. The seven-year-old is completing first grade and has learned to read at about a second grade independent level. The four-year-old has been exposed to books since he was very young and uses this "read-in" time for a "book look." He gathers three to five books, sometimes with adult help, and takes them to the area where everyone else is reading. The seven-year-old is able to read a large number of easy-reading books but still likes to "read" picture books, including wordless ones. A variety of these reading materials are available in the family room for this child. As the family members gather to read, they bring their own reading materials. Anything that "is written that can be read, including comic books" is allowed. When this family gathers, everyone reads his or her choices. They sit in chairs, or lounge on the couch, or sprawl out on the floor on throw pillows.

At the start, it is best to "read-in" for about ten minutes and lengthen the time gradually to twenty to thirty minutes. The children who are not yet reading words can often occupy themselves with picture books and familiar alphabet, counting, and vocabulary books during this period. As the younger children see others absorbed in their books, they will probably be able to busy themselves for a longer time, since that is "the thing to do." If it becomes necessary, the younger children may be dismissed while the older readers complete several chapters. After repeated exposure to this "read-in" process, younger readers and prereaders will be able to take part in the "read-in" for a longer time.

In addition to a regular period of independent reading, it is, we believe, imperative to plan a scheduled family read-aloud session at least once a week or oftener. This is when a "Sustaining Book" might be shared by the entire family. In some families the time for this activity is just before or after the "read-in;" when it follows the "read-in" it serves as bedtime reading for the youngest children. In either case, this is a read-aloud session for all the members of the family.

Bedtime is also a time for your beginning reader to practice her independent reading skills. When a child is encouraged to sit in bed and read for ten minutes, she will begin to build a routine reading habit. Be sure there is good light for reading. Of course, bedtime can also be an appropriate time for you to read aloud to your child or siblings to read to one another. Reading can have a relaxing effect; the child's bedtime might be the favored time for your family to listen to stories and poems. You may also want to try a combination of ten minutes of independent silent reading and ten minutes of reading aloud as an enjoyable way of ending your child's day.

Developing Family Library Habits

The libraries or bookmobiles available in most localities are a source of literature which families should certainly use. In many libraries, programs are available which are designed for the younger child as well as the beginning reader. Film programs, puppet shows, and book talks are among the events usually scheduled.

As your child is beginning to read, it is important that you gradually increase her independence at the library. You might begin by showing her where the "I Can Read" books are, and pointing out particular picture storybooks that have not been selected previously. As your child begins to feel comfortable in the children's part of the library you might go off to the adult sections, telling the child how long you'll be gone and when you'll come back. The length of time you stay away should be flexible; base it on your child's mood and past experience at the library.

When your child feels at home in the library, make certain that he meets one or more of the children's librarians personally. Try to focus the conversation on areas of interest to your child. When your child knows the librarians, he will probably feel free to approach them on his own, ask for necessary help, and perhaps even share the contents of some of the books he has read.

One parent who saw to it that her daughter met the librarian says that now when they go into the library, the librarian will approach the child enthusiastically. "We just got a new book in about snakes, Carrie," he'll say. "You might like it." As he hands her the book, one can almost see Carrie's self-importance grow. Not only has a book been picked out especially for her, but someone remembered her name! For Carrie, the library is a place where she is welcome and where she can learn about things she wants to know. Not surprisingly, she asks to be taken to the library at least once every week. In the meantime, she takes her reading quite seriously. She knows that the librarian, although very busy, will probably find a moment to ask what she thought of the books she is bringing back. If Carrie's parent had not taken the initiative to introduce Carrie to the librarian, it is quite possible tht Carrie would not have the feeling of being a "special somebody" at the library, and consequently not be so interested in the library or its books.

Programs in most libraries vary. Usually a monthly program schedule is available. Place it somewhere in your home where you and your child can see it. Mark off each of the programs you and your child attended with a brightly-colored marker. By making this an important activity, you are reinforcing the value of the offerings at your local library. Library visits should be a scheduled part of each week or bi-weekly period. The more regularly such visits are planned, the more likely it is that your child will begin to form the library habit.

As your child begins to be able to read more easily, you will want to make certain to introduce him to the different sections of the library. Be sure to include the shelves of non-fiction books and the periodicals. If there is a film or filmstrip viewing area, be sure your child knows about it and has access to it. In some libraries, learning games and listening centers are also available. Explore all the possible services your library has to offer. If you see areas that could be enhanced or have suggestions for books to buy, or displays to be constructed, tell the librarian. You can help the library personnel provide a meaningful and worthwhile program not only by letting them know you are pleased with the services offered, but by communicating your needs.

When your child begins to use the library independently, it's a good idea to combine some new responsibility with that independence. Show her how to determine when books are due, make it her job to have all due books ready to take back on each trip to the library. Have it understood that when a book is returned late because the child didn't check the due date, or neglected to take it along, all or part of the fine will be her responsibility. If she has no money of her own, arrange extra chores as payment. This is the best way to accustom a child to getting library books back on time.

Involving Your Child with Literature in Other Ways

Actively involving your child with literature means not only reading a book, but "stretching" it—using it as a base for other activities such as art, drama, or writing. It is important that the parent working with the child be very familiar with the book's content in order to plan the most appropriate activities after a book is read.

A simple "stretching" idea used in one home reinforced the child's confidence in his reading ability and also served as a "talking letter" to his grandparents. At the end of each week, Randy would look through all the books he had read by himself that week and select one favorite chapter or picture storybook to record on tape. When he was satisfied with the tape, it would be sent as the weekly letter to his grandparents who lived some distance away. Their "weekly letter" back to him carried high praise for his reading along with the message that "they couldn't wait to hear the next story!" As Randy became more confident in using the tape recorder, he added sound effects and excerpts of record music where appropriate. What had begun as a simple taping turned into a creative production—one that his grandparents anticipate eagerly.

Examples of a variety of ways to involve your child with literature are presented in the next two sections of this chapter. Although we are advocating these activities in general, it should be noted that they can be overused. There are times when it is appropriate to read and digest a story without having to do something more with it. Also, the suggested activities do not need to be done the same day the story is read. As your child is beginning to read independently that feat in itself may expend most of her energies. You may want to plan an activity with the book the following day. In one family, a particular evening is set aside to do something creative with the books that have been read. The two children select the one book or story read during the week that they liked best. Paper, scissors, crayons, shoeboxes, yarn, and pieces of fabric are on hand, and the children use them in an activity related to the stories. One week the children made a puppet theater and gave an original play. The play was a combination of each child's stories; the various characters met to share adventures and experiences from both. These children were using creative and critical thinking as well as discussion and decision-making skills as they "stretched" beyond their books.

Specific Examples of Using Books with Children

There are many ways that one can involve children with literature. During a second reading of a particular story, family names could be substituted for the written character names. For example, Frog and Toad could become Laurel and Karen (or Mom and Dad). Because Frog and Toad do silly things, the children become quite engrossed in the story and find themselves laughing hilariously at the characters they have become. One can involve the other members of the family in this kind of enjoyable "silly" reading by passing the book around and letting each person read a page, substituting a person's name for each character. Young readers eagerly anticipate hearing their own names used.

This round-family-reading was especially enjoyed by one family in reading the sound books by Peter Spier: *Gobble, Growl, Grunt* [11] and *Crash, Bang, Boom.* [12] For the animal sounds, each person took a turn making the sounds on a particular page. The other family members then guessed which animal was being sounded. The two children, aged 6½ and 8, loved this activity; the letter sounds tickled their tongues! This is also an informal and enjoyable way to reinforce phonics skills.

For *Crash, Bang, Boom*, this family tape-recorded the sounds given by combinations of letters in the book and compared these to the actual sounds. Does the sewing machine really go "Whurra-Whurra-Whur?" Does the vacuum cleaner go "Emmmmmmmmmm?" When the milk is being poured into a glass, does it sound like "clock-clock-clock?" The parents have noted that since beginning this activity, the whole family—even the dog!—seems very aware of the sounds around them. They notice and comment on household sounds such as the noise of brushing teeth, the squeak peculiar to their screen door, and the sound the TV makes as it cools.

Then the family took their "listening ears" outside, carrying a tape recorder along to keep a log of what they heard. After several walks, the eight-year-old read a "Let's-Read-and-Find-Out Science Book" called *The Listening Walk*.[13] The entire family is now in the process of writing their own book, *The Murray's Listening Walk*. The whole family decided what they wanted in the book. They are sharing the taking of photographs. The six-year-old is searching through magazines for illustrations of some sources of sounds not easily photographed at home. The eight-year-old is responsible for the covers and the title page. The parents supplied the materials to make the book and are designing a pocket in the cover for the tape cassette that goes with it. The children have written a script for the tape as well as for the book.

In another family, each of the three children (aged 5½, 7, and 10) have a designated evening after dinner when they read aloud to the family a book or part of a book they particularly like. Although the five-year-old is not truly a "word" reader yet, he gives his interpretations of wordless picture books and picture storybooks. One evening seven-year-old Tony read *Thruway*,[14] an easy-to-read book describing thruways in detail. When Tony finished reading, his father suggested that they build a model thruway. They unanimously decided to make their model a by-pass for Disney World, with the end exit being "Space Mountain." Construction was ingenious with painted toilet paper rolls to hold up the overpasses and bright yellow paint marking the lane dividers on a sturdy cardboard base. The ten-year-old became the landscape architect and suddenly paper trees, flower gardens, and a lakeside rest-stop appeared. The only limit to the project was the size of the original ground board.

Sharing books related to one another either by topic or by author/illustrator can be a growth experience for everyone involved.

The mother of a seven-year-old beginning reader enjoys delving into a subject from many sides and in a depth that one could not get from a single volume. She encouraged her daughter Kristy to choose a topic and then try to find as many books as possible on that topic that she could read. Kristy chose to read about mice and in several cases, rats. The librarian helped Kristy and her mother find beginning level books that featured mice. Among the books Kristy read independently were *Mooch, the Messy*[15] (a rat who kept a sloppy hole begins to change his ways when his father visits); *Noisy Nora*[16] (a mouse who does many noisy things to get her parents' attention, but only succeeds when everything becomes quiet); *Nice New Neighbors*[17] (The Fieldmouse family moves into a new neighborhood. They are not welcomed by the neighborhood children until they all take part in a play created by the Fieldmouse children. The play is "Three Blind Mice," and it has some interesting variations from the standard verses); *The Mouse Book*[18] (a photographically documented story about how real mice find a place for themselves in a house); and *Mouse Soup*[19] (a weasel plans to put a mouse in his soup but is told by the mouse that the soup would be tastier if it contained mouse stories, which he proceeds to tell weasel).

As she completed each story. Kristy drew a picture of the characters or events. The pictures were suspended from a coat hanger to make a "mouse" mobile that was hung in the kitchen where everyone could see it and comment on her mice. Often she labeled the pictures. The mobile also had on it details such as a letter in rat handwriting from *Mooch*.

Kristy also obviously liked the idea of the play in *Nice New Neighbors*. She and several school friends presented the play. Like the animals in the story, Kristy and her friends made up some extra parts so each child would have a role. They made some props and rehearsed the play. Just before the main performance, they helped to make mouse cookies, cut out with a mouse-shaped cookie cutter and individually decorated. As the parents came to pick up their children, they were invited to see a fifteen-minute play (which was repeated) and to munch on a mouse cookie. Making a play based on books that have been read is an idea that a group of parents could oversee cooperatively on a somewhat regular basis.

About two weeks after she completed her mouse mobile, Kristy took it apart and stored the parts in an envelope marked, "Mouse Books, Kristy," and the date. Her mother cleared a drawer in which Kristy could keep her book projects. Kristy made real progress on this topical approach to reading. She is now interested in sea creatures and already has three characters hanging on her new coat hanger mobile.

Focusing upon one author/illustrator's books over a period of one or two months will help the beginning reader notice styles of writing and illustration. With the help of the librarian, one father and his seven-year-old twins, Lonnie and Lucy, decided to read all the books written and illustrated by Ezra Jack Keats.

They began by reading each of the "Peter" books: *A Snowy Day; Whistle for Willie; Peter's Chair; A Letter to Amy; Pet Show;* and *Goggles*. After these titles were read, the trio got all the books together, put them in the order in which they had been published, and opened each to favorite pages. As they went from book to book, they found to their surprise that Peter seemed to grow right before their eyes. They talked about the differences they saw—the length of his pants and the way he was gradually doing more grown-up things. They studied the illustrations and began to see the bits of newspaper, lace, and wallpaper that Keats used in his collages. The three then chose one of the illustrations to see if they could copy Keats's design by cutting out similar shapes of colored paper and gluing them to a piece of cardboard. When they finished, their creation and the page in the book were similar. They were beginning to learn the art of collage.

They each proceeded to choose a different page from one of the books to copy. The latest episode of their collage adventure is to make a family collage book using news clippings, greeting cards, and photographs. They now plan to read more of Keats's works. They also have already chosen about three more authors that they hope to zero in on next!

If you choose to read and study a number of books by a particular author/illustrator, you might introduce your child to the biographical information often found on book jackets. Two volumes that may be available in your public library, *Books Are By People* and *More Books Are By More People* [20], give biographical data about more than 100 children's authors—including Ezra Jack Keats.

In one family, a mother was concerned that her six-year-old daughter Jennifer became frustrated whenever she tried to read "I Can Read" books. The child did have a sizeable sight-vocabulary and a wide speaking vocabulary. She wanted to read books by herself but would quit before she reached the end. Someone suggested that the mother select wordless picture books and let Jennifer tell a story. The mother then wrote down Jenny's words. This is an "at home" adaptation of the Language Experience Approach which is often used as a teaching technique with prereaders and beginning readers.

Jenny often could read the stories when they were written in her own language style. This gave her a feeling of accomplishment and satisfaction. She also was getting practice in story sequence and the specific comprehension of illustrations. With increased practice, she soon included interesting details and gave names to characters. One of the wordless books that she "wrote" was *The Bear and The Fly*.[21] This is the beginning of the story dictated by Jenny to her mother.

> The Bear Family was eating dinner when a fly came in the window. Father Bear got the swatter and hit at the fly. The fly got away but the wine got hit and spilled all over the table.
>
> Father Bear hit at the fly again but he hit Mother Bear's head instead. She looks dead.
>
> But Father Bear keeps chasing the fly. He's mad.

Jenny feels confident reading her own story. Her mother says Jenny often giggles to herself when she reads because the illustrations are so comical. The words she reads are actually more difficult than those in some of the books she found frustrating.

If you do this with your child, type the story if you can.

It will be helpful if you leave wide margins so that there are just a few words on each line.

The more comfortable children like Jenny are with this kind of reading, the easier the transition will be to "I Can Read" books. In fact, they will probably be surprised at just how easy these books are when they go back to them.

Other wordless picture books that have been used successfully with this technique during the beginning-to-read period are *Out! Out! Out!* by Martha Alexander, *Frog Goes To Dinner* by Mercer Mayer, and *April Fools* by Fernando Krahn. If you feel the technique is successful with your child, you might want to progress to more complex wordless books such as *Paddy Pork's Holiday* by John Goodall.

A list of wordless picture books is included here for your reference.

Suggested Wordless Picture Books

Alexander, Martha. *Out! Out! Out!* New York: Dial Press, 1968.

Anno, Mitsumasa. *Topsy, Turvey Pictures to Stretch the Imagination*. New York: Weatherhill, 1970.

Carle, Eric. *I See A Song*. New York: Thomas Y. Crowell, 1973.

Goodall, John S. *The Adventures of Paddy Pork*. New York: Harcourt Brace, 1968.

——. *An Edwardian Christmas*. New York: Atheneum, 1978.

Hutchins, Pat. *Changes, Changes*. New York: Macmillan, 1972.

Krahn, Fernando. *April Fools*. New York: E. P. Dutton, 1974.

——. *Who's Seen the Scissors?* New York: E. P. Dutton, 1975.

Mari, Iela and Enzo. *The Apple and the Moth*. New York: Pantheon, 1970.

Mayer, Mercer. *Ah-Choo*. New York: Dial Press, 1976.

————. *A Boy, A Dog, and A Frog*. New York: Dial Press, 1967.

Schweninger, Ann. *A Dance for Three*. New York: Dial Press, 1979.

Ueno, Noriko. *Elephant Buttons*. New York: Harper & Row, 1973.

Winter, Paula. *The Bear and The Fly*. New York: Crown, 1976.

A Selected Booklist for the Beginning Reader

As was noted at the beginning of this chapter, there are at least three characteristics of books for the beginning reader that parents should look for:

1. A limited amount of print on each page
2. Clear and extensive illustrations
3. The repetition of words and phrases.

The books listed have been selected with these characteristics in mind.

We have also stressed the importance of helping your beginning reader become aware of the many types of books available. Selected samples have been included from the following areas: general "I Can Read" types, science, history, sports, music, poetry and a miscellaneous category.

Books with Minimal Print

Bonsall, Crosby. *The Day I Had to Play with My Baby Sister*. New York: Harper & Row, 1972.

Brother tries to teach younger sister and "pink floppy dog" how to play hide-and-seek.

Topics Covered: Sibling relationships; game rules.

General Involvement: Increase knowledge of games and plan activities, if appropriate, for developing sibling relationships.

Activities: 1) Play a game like "May I" with child(ren). Take turns being the leader. 2) Try variations of hide-and-seek in which hiding would only be allowed near things that start with certain letters. This activity will give your child practice in categorizing. 3) The illustrations are so vivid that they offer many ideas for making a play out of this book. Try to do it enough times so all the character parts can be acted. 4) Cut pictures from magazines showing sibling relationships and mount them on poster board or cardboard. 5) Write a sentence with your child. By arranging pictures and sentences in some sequence, you could make them tell a story.

Burningham, John. *The Baby*. New York: Thomas Y. Crowell, 1974.

In a very simply written book a boy describes his feelings about having a new baby in the house.

Topics Covered: Arrival of a new sibling and the elder child's adaptation to it. Illustrations are helpful in decoding unfamiliar words.

General Involvement: Provide contact with a baby.

Activities: 1) Try to arrange for the child to help feed the baby; discuss with the child what he thinks about babies and feels he can do to help take care of one. 2) Get out the baby pictures of your child or possibly yourself. Together, arrange the photos to tell a story much the way Burningham did. Write down the story; help your child read it. Add names and places. If the story is long divide it with pictures; add a cover and title page; tape, staple, or sew the pages together; display in a place where others will read it. 3) Seek out baby pictures in a magazine; cut them out; mount them on shapes of various colors; attach strings; hang from a coat hanger or other wire shape as a "Baby Face" mobile.

Eastman, P. D. *Go, Dog, Go!* New York: Random House, 1961.

Dogs and more dogs convey the concepts of up, down, and on to the beginning reader. Illustrations add humor as well as provide help with comprehension.

Topics Covered: Directional concepts.

General Involvement: Practice and reinforce conceptual skills.

Activities: 1) Creative drama: act out select pages; copy the dogs' exaggerated actions. 2) Look for directional words such as *in* and *out* on signs in shopping areas. As your child becomes familiar with these words, introduce her to others, such as *exit* and *entrance*. 3) Cut out magazine pictures that represent various concepts or draw some of your interpretations of *in* and *out*. You might both draw your versions of a concept like *under* and then compare them. 4) Play "Follow The Leader" and give directions for some of the activities that the dogs did in the book, such as "Go to that big tree over there." The book *You Go Away* by Dorothy Corey, Chicago: Albert Whitman, 1976, may be used before *Go, Dog, Go!* as it has very little text. Similar concept development activities would apply.

Freschet, Berniece. *Moose Baby*. Illus: Jim Arnosky. New York: G. P. Putnam, 1979.

Moose baby learns a lot in his first year of life.

Topics Covered: Marshlands; skunks; the coyote; a long swim; life of a moose; a bull moose fight.

General Involvement: Learn about the life of a moose.

Activities: 1) Visit a museum or watch a television special on wildlife, especially where animals fight. Discuss reasons for this animal behavior. 2) Study which animals are enemies to which other animals, and ways in which animals seek safety from their enemies.

Himler, Ronald. *Wake Up, Jeremiah*. New York: Harper & Row, 1979.

Jeremiah arises before his parents to see the sun rise at the top of the hill.

Topics Covered: Sunrise.

General Involvement: Talk about experiences of getting up before dawn or before parents arise.

Activities: 1) Plan to wake up very early one morning to see the sun rise. 2) Experiment with ways of drawing and painting a sunrise.

Hutchins, Pat. *Titch*. New York: Macmillan, 1971.

Titch is not old or big enough to do the things his siblings do but he can plant a seed that grows and grows.

Topics Covered: Sibling age differences and capabilities; planting of seeds.

General Involvement: Talk with your youngest child about how he feels as the baby in the family; plant some seeds.

Activities: 1) Find a variety of seed samples including those from plants that produce their own seeds; plant the seeds; make a chart plotting their growth. 2) Invite members of your family or your child's playmates to pantomime the story of *Titch*. 3) The pantomime might grow into creative drama where the players speak the parts and use props of three different sizes. As the story becomes familiar, encourage players to exchange roles so each can better understand Titch. Plant a real seed at the end of the play that the players can actually watch grow!

Minarik, Else Holmelund. *Cat and Dog.* Illus: Fritz Siebel. New York: Harper & Row, 1960.

A cat and dog skirmish hilariously in and out of the house. Finally, the girl who owns them feeds them and finds a peaceable solution.

Topics Covered: Behavior and care of pets.

General Involvement: Expose child to variety of animals; note care.

Activities: 1) If you have a pet, make a list with your child of the care it requires; read the list; number the things on the list in the order of their importance; put the list where your child can read it independently. 2) Read the story aloud again. Change the characters by making the cat a giraffe and the dog an elephant. Enjoy this silly story together. Your child may want to illustrate this new story. 3) If possible, try to visit a local veterinarian. He or she may take time to show you the kennels and the equipment used to treat animals. Perhaps your child could listen to a dog's heartbeat. 4) When you go to the grocery store, examine the many kinds of pet foods commercially available. Together, read some of the can labels. Think about how the ingredients of canned pet food compare to the "bone" fought over in the story.

Myers, Bernice. *Come Out, Shadow, Wherever You Are!* New York: Scholastic Book Services, 1970.

Davy discovers shadows and is called a copy cat when he follows in someone else's shadow. Then he finds that even he has a shadow and that it will do whatever he wants it to.

Topics Covered: Shadows; independence; self-exploration.

General Involvement: Explore environment with the purpose of discovering all kinds of shadows.

Activities: 1) Supply your child with a flashlight and together make shadows on the walls—a great rainy day activity. 2) Look for shadows at different times of the day; ask your librarian for a book that will help you and your child learn why shadows are sometimes long and sometimes short. See if you and your child can hypothesize about why your shadows change size, then go outside at different times to test your hypothesis. This is one way to help direct your child in the experience of problem solving. 3) Invent shadow games: trying to avoid stepping on another's shadow, racing your shadows, dramatizing animal shadow motions like a sluggish elephant with a long trunk, playing Follow the Leader, making your shadow do things the leader's shadow does.

Perkins, Al. *The Ear Book*. Illus: William O'Brien. New York: Random House, 1968.

A very simple concept book about the sounds the ear hears. Humorous illustrations; basic words used repeatedly.

Topics Covered: General sounds in the environment.

General Involvement: Help the child to a greater awareness that "ears hear."

Activities: 1) Walk with your child in the neighborhood; if possible carry a tape recorder to record sounds heard. When you return home, list all the things you and the child remember hearing—then replay the tape to check against the list. 2) Imitate sounds of things, animals, and people; add dramatic actions; try to guess what sounds the other is imitating. 3) Read the book together in a normal tone of

voice except for the actual noise words like "tick,
tock," or "drop, drop, drop." Say those words exceptionally loud or exceptionally softly. You also can
read the words fast one time (ticktockticktock) and
slowly the next (t-i-c-k t-o-c-k, t-i-c-k t-o-c-k).

Dr. Seuss. *Hop on Pop*. New York: Random House, 1963.
A nonsensical approach to word families (sad, bad,
dad, had) that should help increase your beginning
reader's reading confidence.

Topics Covered: Word families; concepts about
feelings, size, and directions.

General Involvement: Help the child be sure he
knows these words by sight. Read the end pages too!

Activities: 1) After the book is read, say one of the
words and see if the child can remember the other
words in that family that are in the story. Then see if
you can both name additional ones. Make a list with
a bright-colored magic marker. 2) Check your child's
comprehension by seeing if she can remember how
a word (such as *hop*) was used. 3) Make up your own
silly rhymes using the family word groups given in
the book or other family groups; write the rhymes;
read them together as fast as you can. It's delightful
tongue-twisting fun!

Tether, Graham. *Skunk and Possum*. Illus: Lucinda
McQueen. Boston: Houghton Mifflin, 1979.
There are four episodes (chapters) in this book telling the tales of silly Skunk and her wise, tactful
friend, Possum. Skunk makes perfume, paints a portrait, plays the tuba, and goes on a picnic. The
stories are simply written to make good, humorous
beginning reading materials.

Topics Covered: Making perfume; painting a portrait; playing the tuba; and going on a picnic.

General Involvement: Help your child learn

about tact—when to be entirely honest and when to consider the feelings of a friend.

Activities: 1) Parallel to the story, you might try to make some perfume from flower petals after reading how that is done. Visit a perfume counter in a department store and smell all the different scents. 2) Visit a portrait painter and watch as the artist paints a portrait. Study silhouettes and faces, and try drawing them from different perspectives. 3) Attend a band concert, or a parade, or visit a music store and point out the tubas. 4) Go on a picnic.

Each of the books in the Minimal Print group contains clear, explicit illustrations. The amount of print, however, is generally more limited in these than in the next group of books.

Books with Clear and Extensive Illustrations

Gackenbach, Dick. *Hattie Be Quiet, Hattie Be Good*. New York: Harper & Row, 1977.
An "Early I Can Read" book written in two chapters that features Hattie trying to do housework, enduring an hour of quiet, and caring for a sick friend—as well as enjoying "chocolate almond delight" ice cream.
Topics Covered: Trying to do grown-up things; realizing how long an hour is; caring for someone who does not feel well.
General Involvement: Help your child experience grown-up work and learn about length of time. The character provides a model for taking care of the ill.
Activities: 1) Place some of the home cleaning tools, such as a vacuum cleaner, within your child's reach; first show him how to use it; designate a spe-

cific piece of carpet or part of room that the child is responsible for cleaning (if possible, let the child help decide where to clean). 2) Whenever you finish an activity together, such as reading a story, going to the park, or taking a bath, mention how long it took. Say, "That took 15 minutes," or "That took half an hour." The repetitive comments about the length of time spent doing things should help your child better comprehend this rather abstract concept. 3) Have a contest with your child to see just how long each of you can be quiet. 4) Teach your child to make a simple recipe. Work on doing a non-cooking breakfast recipe together. When the recipe has been mastered, put all the ingredients in a place she can reach. Help her plan to make and serve breakfast to you in bed. 5) If a friend is ill, together plan something special to do for him or her. Be certain your child is in on the decision-making. Perhaps she can draw a picture of Hattie taking care of her friend, and of their eating ice cream together.

Garelick, May. *Just Suppose*. Illus: Brinton Turkle. New York: Scholastic Book Services, 1969.

A creative dramatization approach to acting out the actions and making the sounds of various animals—a monkey, a fish, and a hungry lion.

Topics Covered: Actions and sounds of a number of animals.

General Involvement: Imitate the animals presented (actually make the pages of the book come alive).

Activities: 1) After the book is read, go over it page by page with one person reading and the others acting out the animals. Read another time, putting adjectives before the actions, such as "huge," "sluggish," or "speedy" to add variation and dimension to the action. 2) Follow the book's suggestion to dramatize other animals not specifically illustrated in the book. 3) Draw pictures of how each of you looks imitating various animals. 4) Record the sounds made while imitating the animals; write an "animal script" and have listeners guess from the sounds just which animal is being imitated. 5) Bake animal cookies (using cookie cutters) and then feed them to the "pretend animals" at your house. They must say "Thank you" using the animal's voice. 6) Play Saint-Saen's "Carnival of the Animals;" improvise a dance putting the various actions of the animals to the rhythm and tempo of the music.

Guilfoile, Elizabeth. *Nobody Listens to Andrew*. Illus: Mary Stevens. Chicago: Follett, 1957.

Andrew tries to get everyone's attention but only succeeds when he announces that there is a bear in his bed!

Topics Covered: Attention paid to others; community helpers; bear's habits.

General Involvement: Become aware of the listening habits of your family at home.

Activities: 1) Say something, have the others in the room repeat it; make messages longer and longer; key in on exact listening. 2) Help your child learn what to do if there is an emergency in your home. Talk about the specific community helpers in your area. Practice dialing their telephone numbers (with the receiver down). Let your child practice reading a list of emergency telephone numbers. 3) Take your child to open house at the fire house and police station.

Hill, Donna. *Ms. Glee Was Waiting*. Illus: Diane Dawson. New York: Atheneum, 1978.

The efforts of Laura to get to her piano lesson include a ride on a wagon, a bus, a tugboat, a balloon, and even an elephant howdah. Interesting vocabulary, an imaginative story, and a practical situation most children face—getting somewhere on time.

Topics Covered: Getting somewhere on time; different modes of transportation.

General Involvement: Notice different types of transportation; learn to tell time.

Activities: 1) Make a calendar to put on your refrigerator which indicates when lessons and other events will occur. 2) Set alarms or timers to remind you and your child when it is time to do things. 3) Collect pictures of unusual types of transportation to put in a scrapbook.

Keats, Ezra Jack. *Jennie's Hat*. New York: Harper & Row, 1966.

Jenny's aunt sends her a hat, which is plain and not decorated with flowers and berries as Jenny hoped it would be. She envisions all sorts of decorating ideas for it but is finally satisfied when some birds in the park decorate it with a nest and flowers.

Topics Covered: Decorating objects; environmental "finds;" and something about birds' nests. (Even though only slight mention of this last topic is made in the book, it is enough to act as a springboard for developing the subject.)

General Involvement: Provide opportunities for decorating; help your child become more aware both of birds' nests and of collage materials to be found in the environment.

Activities: 1) Find something "plain" in your house, such as a hat, a lampshade, or a wastebasket, which could be perked up with decorations. Have a scavenger hunt in the house for bits and pieces of ribbon, swatches of material, and used greeting cards. Enjoy making a collage together and decorating the object you have selected. 2) Do a team search in your neighborhood to see if you can find materials similar to the ones used in the book. 3) While searching for things, you might also look for and count all the birds' nests in the neighborhood. Discuss with your child the likenesses and differences among the nests. You might read aloud a "Let's-Read-and-Find-Out Science Book" published by Thomas Y. Crowell entitled *It's Nesting Time*.

Keats, Ezra Jack. *Maggie and the Pirates*. New York: Four Winds Press, 1979.

Joey, the boy who stole Maggie's cricket and cage, returns the cage and catches a new cricket after hers had died. This story might frighten little children, but it handles the topics of honesty and death very realistically and gently.

Topics Covered: Death of a pet; honesty and stealing.

General Involvement: Discuss when an item has been stolen, or when a pet has died.

Activities: 1) Read and talk about the child's feelings when something has been stolen or when a pet has died. 2) Build a cage for a cricket or some other animal.

McLeod, Emilie Warren. *The Bear's Bicycle*. Illus: David McPhail. Boston: Little, Brown, 1975.

The book follows a boy on his bicycle through a town during the course of a day. Bicycle do's and don'ts are presented in the text. Humor appears in the illustrations as a huge bear does everything catastrophically and hilariously wrong!

Topics Covered: Bicycle safety.

General Involvement: Provide actual examples of how a bicycle rider should behave.

Activities: 1) Pantomime the story; first the bear's

part, then the boy's part; later, two people may do the parts together. 2) Draw a poster that demonstrates a specific bicycle safety rule; display it on the refrigerator. 3) Because the bear's message is not written in words, help your child to compare the bear's and boy's actions orally. 4) This story is an excellent choice for a child to read aloud during the family "Sustaining Book" time. Be certain everyone looks at the delightful illustrations. 5) Provide the materials so that the surprise ending can be reenacted at your house: milk, crackers, and a teddy bear!

Miles, Miska. *Chicken Forgets*. Boston: Little, Brown, 1976.

A mother hen sends her chick to fetch a basket of blackberries and clearly warns him not to forget what to bring. After several detours and memory lapses, the chick comes back with a basket of berries and an increased pride in himself.

Topics Covered: Stresses how important it is to follow through on an expected task.

General Involvement: Help your child become familiar with different kinds of berries.

Activities: 1) Role-play the story by letting your child be the chicken and your taking the part of the other animal characters; then invent a similar story of your own. 2) If possible, introduce your child to blackberries; eat some plain and bake some in a pie or tart; talk about the different way the berries taste when raw and when cooked. 3) Assign a task to your child, such as borrowing an egg from a neighbor. (Prearrange the borrowing with a phone call.) Decide on a route for the errand that will have many inviting distractions. The challenge for your child is to stay at the task. Reverse this; let your child instruct you to do a task that you had better not forget!

Rice, Eve. *Sam Who Never Forgets*. New York: Greenwillow, 1977.

As Sam, the zookeeper, distributes food to the animals in the zoo, the elephant thinks he has been forgotten because Sam keeps passing him by with partial wagonloads of food. In the end, elephant gets a whole wagonload of his own.

Topics Covered: Animal food and zoo feeding activity; zookeeper's duties.

General Involvement: Help the child to understand more about zoo animals and their food.

Activities: 1) Visit a zoo; some zoos give special tours or will at least inform you of feeding hours. 2) Do a "zoo food hunt" in the grocery store to find any of the foods the zoo animals might eat; if so, buy some of the finds for a "zoo tasting party." 3) Talk with your child about the food of other zoo animals not mentioned in the book. 4) Pretend you and your child are zookeepers; role-play your tasks. One of you could be a zookeeper while the other played the part of an elephant, a kangaroo, or some other animal.

Books with Repetition of Words and Phrases

Heilbroner, Joan. *This is the House Where Jack Lives*. Illus: Aliki. New York: Harper & Row, 1962.

The popular cumulative nursery rhyme, "The House That Jack Built," is given a modern apartment house twist in this version. Illustrations are full of humor and will aid comprehension.

Topics Covered: Silly possibilities of what might happen to someone who lives in an apartment house.

General Involvement: See if your child is familiar with apartment houses. Help him understand the accumulative aspect of this story.

Activities: 1) Compare the apartment house events in this story with what might really happen in apartment houses your child knows or will be taken to. Point out differences: some have elevators or balconies, for example; others do not. 2) Read "The House That Jack Built." You may need to define such words as *malt*. Reread the book and contrast the events and styles of the two stories. How are they alike, how different? Which one does your child like best? Why? Ask her to show you the place in the book she likes best and to read it aloud to you. 3) Select one of the stories to read again. As the story culminates, read louder. You should be shouting at the end. Or do it in reverse, shouting at the beginning and whispering at the end. 4) Draw pictures of cumulative things you would want to happen in your apartment house. 5) Cut pictures of different apartment houses from magazines; glue to poster board to make an apartment house collage. 6) Construct an apartment house out of blocks or shoeboxes and other odds and ends. Use your imagination in representing the windows, balconies, chimneys, and other apartment house features.

Baum, Arline and Joseph. *One Bright Monday Morning*. New York: Random House, 1962.

A cumulative concept book that starts out "One bright Monday morning while on my way to school, I saw 1 blade of green grass growing near a little blue pool." Flowers, birds, and animals are added each day of the week to furnish all the signs of *spring*!

Topics Covered: Days of the week, weather, signs of spring.

General Involvement: Observation; practice in observing weather signs and days of the week.

Activities: 1) Have child read this book about two weeks prior to a "visible spring" in your area. Then together, keep a *diary* (buy an inexpensive one—maybe even one with a key) following the format of the book: One (weather word) (day) (time of day) on my way to _____ I saw _____. The next day write the same sentence again on a second page but add one more observation. You should have a filled diary when spring is in full regalia. 2) Adapt this idea to the anticipatory signs of summer, autumn, and winter.

Charlip, Remy. *Fortunately*. New York: Parents' Magazine Press, 1964.

A humorous book about the adventures and misadventures of a New York boy who tries to get to a birthday party in Florida. Uncluttered, helpful illustrations, minimal text. The words, "Fortunately" or "Unfortunately" begin each page.

Topics Covered: Good luck and bad luck; birthday parties.

General Involvement: Offer your child practice in prediction; encourage imaginative thinking.

Activities: 1) Talk with your child about the pattern or repetition of the book; dramatize several of the unfortunately–fortunately combinations. 2) Clip pictures from magazines. Find something "fortunate" or "unfortunate" in each picture. For example, someone in the picture is looking at a mysteriously half-eaten cake that was meant for a party. That is "unfortunate". "Fortunately," there are six more cakes in the oven! 3) Make a booklet with the magazine pictures, writing the comments you and your child have made about them; read the finished product together.

Galdone, Paul. *The Old Woman and Her Pig*. New York: McGraw-Hill, 1960.

In this folktale an old woman finds a sixpence and decides to buy a pig. Her troubles begin! The pig won't get over the stile and the woman cries "I shan't get home tonight." This is repeated over and over as she unsuccessfully tries to enlist the help of a dog, a stick, fire, water, a rope, and a rat in this humorous cumulative tale—which reverses, resulting in a solution to the problem.

Topics Covered: Giving something (in the book, a saucer of milk for the cat) in exchange for help may get results.

General Involvement: Have fun with oral language; help, in a humorous way, to clarify for your child the idea of cause and effect.

Activities: 1) Read the tale aloud together, putting in stubborn "no's" for the animals who refuse to help. As the cat begins to kill the rat, read faster until you are almost out of breath at the end and can heave a relieved sigh when the old woman gets home. 2) Practice reading the story several times; perhaps adding sound effects such as the rat's gnawing of the rope, the crackling of fire, and the splashing of water. Tape record your oral version of this tale. Send the cassette to a special relative or friend. 3) This story is fun for a group of children to dramatize during an "I have nothing to do" time. Help them make a list of the props they need: a rope, stuffed toy pig, a stick. They could present their play to their parents. 4) Make up an original "Old Lady" story. She might start out by finding a bag of gold pieces! Try to think of all the cumulative crazy things that could happen if she started by buying something like a Rolls Royce that won't go, for example. 5) Give your child a task, but also trade something for it or reward her in return. For example, if she dusts all the chairs, you will do one of her regular jobs.

Dr. Seuss. *Green Eggs and Ham*. New York: Random House, 1960.

Sam-I-Am tries to convince a Dr. Seuss character to like Green Eggs and Ham—a phrase repeated often. After being nagged repeatedly, the character tries the dish, and reiterates the entire story ending

"I do like green eggs and ham.
　　　　Thank you.
　　　　Thank you.
　　　　Sam-I-Am!"

Topics Covered: Prejudging something.

General Involvement: Expose the child to a variety of new experiences.

Activities: 1) Introduce a new vegetable; make it attractive; try it together; let the child help you buy and prepare it. 2) Go with your child to the supermarket and seek out foods your family has not tried—at least not in his experience. Buy one new item each time you shop. 3) After your child is braver at experimenting, visit the gourmet section of the store and select something even more unusual; perhaps some imported food. 4) If you are brave, invent your own version of Green Eggs and Ham.

Many of the following books satisfy the previous requirements of limited print, clear illustrations, and repetition. We are including both books that exemplify certain characteristics of format and style and those that are appropriate because of their content. We hope this dual listing will help you to become more aware of specific characteristics of books suitable for the beginning reader as well as encourage you to introduce your child to a wide variety of the books available for her to read.

General Books for the Beginning Reader

Anderson, Hans Christian. *Thumbelina*. Translated by Amy Ehrlich. Illus: Susan Jeffers. New York: Dial Press, 1979.

The beautiful, large illustrations accompanying this classic Anderson tale make browsing through the book like walking through an art gallery. Read this aloud to a beginning reader.

Topics Covered: Storytelling; size relationships.

General Involvement: Look at things from different perspectives.

Activities: 1) Compare these illustrations with those in other books illustrated by Susan Jeffers. 2) Compare different versions of the Thumbelina story. 3) Talk about what the world looks like to an ant, a bee, a giant, and other creatures of different sizes.

Lobel, Arnold. *Frog and Toad All Year*. (An I Can Read Book). New York: Harper & Row, 1976.

Five spritely told stories relate the seasonal adventures of Frog and Toad: "Down The Hill" (sledding in the winter); "The Corner" (looking for the corner that "Spring is just around"); "Ice Cream" (on a summer day, Toad becomes covered with chocolate ice cream and can't be recognized); "The Surprise" (Frog and Toad each rake the other's autumn leaves as a surprise—but the wind changes all that); and "Christmas Eve" (Frog is late and Toad is worried).

Topics Covered: The seasons; caring about another; taking words literally.

General Involvement: Help your child become better aware of the four seasons.

Activities: 1) Select one snapshot of yourself or your child taken during each of the four seasons; think about what you might have been doing then; make up a story much like the Frog and Toad tales; write it; illustrate each story imaginatively (use pieces of cotton for snow, actual seeds glued to a page for seeds to be planted,); bind the story into a booklet; be certain to include your child's name in the title, the way Frog and Toad were. 2) Try to get a calendar with clearly seasonal illustrations; go through the calendar marking special family days and holidays; discuss the illustration for that month; help your child understand why that particular illustration was used. 3) With your child, design your own calendar; the illustrations could include seasonal family photographs. 4) Take a family vote on favorite seasons and months; ask each member of the family to give specific reasons for his or her choice.

Parish, Peggy. *Teach Us, Amelia Bedelia*. (A Read-Alone Book). Illus: Lynn Sweat. New York: Greenwillow, 1977.

Amelia Bedelia's literal interpretation of words and phrases goes into the classroom as Amelia unintentionally becomes the substitute teacher. She is delightfully zany as she plants light bulbs, paints pictures that are already drawn, and takes everyone to the Rogers's home to pick apples for counting practice.

Topics Covered: Words with multiple meanings; one-to-one correspondence; making taffy apples.

General Involvement: Expose the child to words with more than one meaning.

Activities: 1) Write a word on paper or on a 3 × 5

card. On the back, write a sentence using the word but don't let your child see it; ask him to define the word, then turn the card over and together compare his definition to the way it is used in your sentence. If you and the child choose the same meaning, call attention to other meanings. Then reverse roles and have him select the word, write the sentence, and ask you for a definition. 2) Go to a grocery store or orchard (preferably) to buy or pick apples for taffy apples; find a recipe or use the simple recipe for candied apples in *The Joy of Cooking* (Rombauer and Becker; Bobbs-Merrill, 1931).

Van Woerkom, Dorothy O. *Harry and Shellburt*. (Ready To Read). Illus: Erick Ingraham. New York: Macmillan, 1977.

Harry the hare and Shellburt the tortoise decide to reenact Aesop's tortoise-hare race. Harry vows it won't end the same way again! They race to the cabbage patch. When Harry reaches it, there is no sign of Shellburt, so he takes a nap and is outwitted by the tortoise. They enjoy a cabbage salad— complete with flies for Shellburt.

Topics Covered: Aesop's fable; differences of "speed" among animals; salads; sportsmanship.

General Involvement: Be certain your child knows what a hare and tortoise are, and about races and salads as well.

Activities: 1) Read Aesop's "The Tortoise and the Hare"; together with your child, contrast and compare the two "fables." 2) Set up a race either for yourselves or with different animals. This involves making decisions about how long it should be, where, what prizes will be offered. 3) Let your child help make a salad for dinner and be in charge of selecting a dressing for the salad from several choices. We trust you will make your salad *without* flies!

History

Baker, Betty. *Little Runner at the Longhouse*. (An I Can Read Book). New York: Harper & Row, 1962.

A story of the warm interaction between an Indian boy and his mother. Details of New Year traditions are presented.

Topics Covered: Longhouse living, maple sugar; harvest time; wampum; New Year's celebration; responsibility of children.

General Involvement: Discuss the topic of American Indians with your child to see what concepts he holds. You might want to try to rectify possible misconceptions.

Activities: 1) Find words in the book, such as *wampum*, and ask your child to tell what our equivalent of it is—*money*. 2) Attend a "sugaring-off," if you can find one in the area where you live; encourage your child to taste maple sugar. 3) Compare the New Year's traditions in the story with the way you celebrate the New Year in your home. 4) Play a "trade" game with your child similar to the one played in the story.

Hall, Donald. *The Ox Cart Man*. Illus: Barbara Cooney. New York: Viking, 1979.

This lyrical tale of a man's journey to Portsmouth Market in nineteenth-century New England is enchanting. A very realistic, historical presentation of family life is given, with few words on a page.

Topics Covered: Seasons; family roles in nineteenth-century New England; market.

General Involvement: Talk about how families

lived in historical times; discuss the meaning of unfamiliar terms.

Activities: 1) Visit a farmer's market. 2) Visit an historical museum like Cooperstown, Upper Canada Village, Sturbridge Village. 3) Learn to whittle, embroider, weave.

Lowery, Janette Sebring. *Six Silver Spoons*. (An I Can Read History Book). Illus: Robert Quackenbush. New York: Harper & Row, 1971.

Tells of the British leaving colonial Boston for Concord and the story of how a young girl and her brother that evening safely carry to Lexington six silver spoons made by Paul Revere. During the story, Revere issues his famous warning.

Topics Covered: Revolutionary War; family affection.

General Involvement: Help the child form an accurate concept of the American Revolution and how people who lived in the towns were affected.

Activities: 1) Read Longfellow's poem, "The Midnight Ride of Paul Revere". 2) Study maps together to see where the war took place and especially where Concord, Lexington, and Boston are located. 3) Unpack and examine any 1976 Bicentennial memorabilia you may have; recall how your community celebrated that July 4th; explain to your child why; find out what, if anything, your child remembers about the Bicentennial. 4) Play marching music; pantomime the marching of the soldiers. 5) Visit a department store (or possibly a local silversmith) to examine silverware.

Monjo, F. N. *The Drinking Gourd*. (An I Can Read History Book). New York: Harper & Row, 1970.

Tommy's father helps runaway slaves, guided by the Big Dipper or the "Drinking Gourd," reach the underground railroad that will take them to freedom in Canada.

Topics Covered: Slavery; underground railroad; Big Dipper; constellations; gourds.

General Involvement: Be certain your child has an accurate concept of the words *slavery* and *constellation*.

Activities: 1) On a map of the United States, trace routes that could have been taken from the abolition states to Canada. 2) Take your child to the grocery store or to a farm in the fall. Encourage her to hold and examine the various kinds of gourds. 3) Take a night walk to hunt for the Big Dipper, the Little Dipper, and other constellations. Talk about why your child thinks the Big Dipper might have been called "the Drinking Gourd."

Science

Goffstein, M. B. *Natural History*. New York: Farrar, Straus and Giroux, 1979.

This small book contains few words, but a powerful message about ecological relationships. "Every living creature is our brother and our sister," it says at one point.

Topics Covered: Ecology; humanitarian behavior.

General Involvement: Help your child learn how not to be wasteful, how to preserve resources, to conserve energy, and to treasure all living things.

Activities: Explore the activities of such organizations as the Audubon Society, Friends of Animals, etc. 2) Visit your local Humane Society. 3) Observe, take pictures of, draw (but do not touch or harm) insects and small animals that live near you.

Goldin, Augusta. *Spider Silk*. (A Let's-Read-And-Find-

Out Science Book.) Illus: Joseph Low. New York: Thomas Y. Crowell, 1964.

The many attributes of spider webs found both in and outside the home are presented in a clear, informative manner.

Topics Covered: Specific and accurate information about spiders, with emphasis on the spinning of webs.

General Involvement: Help your child be aware of spider webs.

Activities: 1) Observe webs, without destroying them, in as many ways and places as possible; use a magnifying glass. 2) Try to watch one particular spider for a period of one week; look for signs of an egg sac, note how the web enlarges, observe what the spider does when she detects that someone or something is near. 3) Visit a local weaver; find out about the kinds of spinning equipment used by people; compare the spider's delicate weaving to that done by human hands or machine. 4) Observe a web right after a rain or when the morning dew is still on it making it seem to sparkle. 5) Photograph webs; let your child do some of the actual photographing; when the film is developed, write a description or caption for each photo. 6) Cut paper strips, 1″ × 12″, and show your child how to weave a construction paper placemat. 7) Enjoy the fingerplay, "Eency Weency Spider" or role-play the nursery rhyme, "Little Miss Muffet". Even the older beginning reader likes to review some of the old, familiar rhymes. 8) Select *Charlotte's Web* as a "Sustaining Book" to read aloud. (E. B. White, Harper & Row, 1952).

Norris, Louanne, and Howard E. Smith. *An Oak Tree Dies and a Journey Begins*. Illus: Allen Davis. New York: Crown, 1979.

In black and white sketches the reader follows all of the interesting things that happen after an oak tree dies.

Topics Covered: Natural history; decay; life cycles.

General Involvement: Learn about what happens to dead trees.

Activities: 1) Visit a woodland, a park, or a forest and observe the many uses to which dead vegetation is being put. 2) Visit a museum to study the life cycles of vegetation. 3) Study different types of trees and compare them.

Selsam, Millicent. *Plenty of Fish*. (An I Can Read Science Book). New York: Harper & Row, 1960.

A boy buys goldfish and a bowl and learns about the care of these pets including how they breathe and their habits.

Topics Covered: Fish; food; gills; breathing; the relationship of plants and oxygen.

General Involvement: Help your child become aware of the many pets available and the care and accessories necessary for each.

Activities: 1) Visit a pet store with your child. 2) Observe how various animals breathe. 3) Observe your child doing the breathing exercises demonstrated in the book.

Wyler, Rose and Gerald Ames. *Prove It!* (An I Can Read Science Book). New York: Harper & Row, 1963.

This is a science involvement book in easy-to-read format. Experiments include those with air, water, sound, and magnets.

Topics Covered: Air; water; sound; magnets.

General Involvements: Help your child practice following directions in order to complete an experiment successfully. Together find the necessary materials for the experiment, which should be available in most homes.

Activities: 1) With your child, choose several of the experiments and perform them. 2) Encourage the child to complete one or more experiments independently; as a summary, ask her to explain the procedure and results to you. 3) Locate other simple experiment books in the library and select experiments from them to do together or independently.

Mystery

Bonsall, Crosby. *The Case of the Hungry Stranger*. (An I Can Read Mystery). New York: Harper & Row, 1963.
Mrs. Much's blueberry pie has disappeared. She asks Wizard and his friends to find out who took it.
Topics Covered: Baking; disappearance; clubhouses; the way certain foods discolor the teeth.
General Involvement: See if your child knows what blueberries and clubhouses are.
Activities: 1) Eat a variety of vegetables and fruits; see if lips or teeth become discolored (include at least one, such as blueberries, that does). 2) Bake a favorite dessert together; encourage your child to read the directions to you.

Lexau, Joan M. *The Rooftop Mystery*. (An I Can Read Mystery). Illus: Syd Hoff. New York: Harper & Row 1968.
Two boys feel silly carrying a sister's "huge" doll. They leave it on the rooftop while they look for someone else to carry it. When they return to the roof, the doll is missing! After several searches, the mystery is solved.
Topics Covered: Moving; helping family members; rooftop clotheslines; leaving objects unattended; embarrassment.
General Involvement: Help child understand

about the confusions that can occur on moving day, and that a boy carrying a doll is not silly; offer a guide to what to do if one of the child's possessions disappear.

Activities: 1) Observe a neighbor moving; discuss some of the confusions that took place; discuss how people helped one another. 2) If possible, take your child to the top of an apartment building; observe what is there: clothesline, chimneys, flower gardens. 3) Think together about some of the things you or your child would feel foolish doing; pretend to or actually do several of the most appropriate activities together. 4) Look carefully at the organization of the story; pick out the incidents that make it a mystery (i.e. disappearance, search); use these elements to write or tell your own mysteries; you might use a family name in the title: "The Strange Happenings on the Madison's Front Porch".

Sharmat, Marjorie. *Nate The Great and the Phony Clue*. New York: Coward-McCann, and Geoghegan, 1977. Nate The Great and his dog, Sludge, solve a mystery involving a torn paper note.

Topics Covered: Alphabet; word parts; reading writing on wet paper; writing notes; detectives.

General Involvement: See how hard it is to read messages or labels with missing parts.

Activities: 1) Write a note; tear it into pieces; try to have your child put it back together and read it; reverse the procedure by having your child write the note. 2) Wet paper and try to read the message from the back side of the paper.

Thayer, Jane. *Where Is Squirrel?* Illus: Bari Weissman. New York: William Morrow, 1979. This is a simple detective story with animal characters.

Topics Covered: The disappearance of squirrel.

General Involvement: Try to figure out where squirrel is.

Activities: 1) Study clues—make up your own detective stories. 2) Try to predict the outcome.

Sports

Kessler, Leonard. *On Your Mark, Get Set, Go! The First All-Animal Olympics*. (An I Can Read Sports Book). New York: Harper & Row, 1972.

A group of hard working and thinking animals stage their own Olympic Games. Owl is the self-appointed coach.

Topics Covered: Olympics; game rules; exercising; competition.

General Involvement: Help your child become more aware of the scope of the Olympic Games.

Activities: 1) If an Olympic year, or when other competition activities are televised, watch a variety of the scheduled events with your child. 2) Help your child organize a relay race; provide different relay objects. 3) Many Olympic winners appear on television periodically; point out these personalities to your child; discuss the event or events that each won. 4) Plan a neighborhood Olympics; it could be combined with a block party. Make special ribbons or medals so that everyone will be a "winner!"

Krementz, Jill. *A Very Young Gymnast*. New York: Alfred A. Knopf, 1978.

A young gymnast's life is portrayed as she is in training and as a competitor. The text may require team reading. However, the photographs are quite descriptive and detailed. They will provide your child the opportunity for careful picture reading.

Topics Covered: Exercises; gymnastic training and competition.

General Involvement: Help your child understand the rigor required to become a capable gymnast.

Activities: 1) Attend a gymnastic meet. 2) Watch gymnastic events together on TV. 3) After warming up, try some of the simpler exercises shown in the book. 4) A "Sustaining Book" choice might be to read a biography of an accomplished young gymnast.

Phleger, F. and M. *Off To The Races*. (I Can Read It By Myself Beginner Book). New York: Random House, 1968.

A younger brother follows his older brother to a bicycle rally and actually enters a race and places second.

Topics Covered: Bicycle racing; competition; hostels; types of bikes.

General Involvement: Help your child learn more about bicycles through observation and participation.

Activities: 1) Visit a museum where unicycles and other types of cycles are displayed; discuss and compare cycles. 2) Attend a bike race or point out racers you might see on the road. 3) Enjoy a bike ride together.

Music

Brand, Oscar. *When I First Came To This Land*. New York: G. P. Putnam, 1974.

"But the land was sweet and good, and I did what I could," is the familiar refrain of the folk song featured in this picture book. It is silly at times and yet reflects the pioneer spirit.

Topics Covered: Pioneer life; rhyming; naming things.

General Involvement: Help child to have fun with rhyming words.

Activities: 1) Sing the song using the music in the book. 2) Take turns singing the verses but omitting an end rhyme word; let the listener sing the rhyme word. 3) Sing the song faster and faster until the words twist your tongue!

Isadora, Rachel. *Ben's Trumpet*. New York: Greenwillow, 1979.

The black, silver, and white silhouettes of this unusual book impart the feeling of jazz music perfectly. A young child passes some jazz players at rehearsal daily. Ben gets to try a real trumpet only after hours of pretending to play one of his own, and after other children make fun of him for pretending.

Topics Covered: Jazz; musical instruments; pretending; really wanting something; children making fun of you.

General Involvement: Listen to jazz music.

Activities: 1) Attend a jazz band concert or listen to a record or cassette tape recording of jazz music. 2) Learn to identify brass instruments by sight and by sound. 3) Talk about children who make fun of other children. 4) Pantomime the playing of different musical instruments.

Spier, Peter. *The Fox Went Out On a Chilly Night*. Garden City, N.Y.: Doubleday, 1961.

A fox invades a town and manages to "catch a goose" to take back to his den-o! A repetitive, easy-to-read folk song with the music included.

Topics Covered: Animals prey on others; fox lives in a den (although the den is not pictured realistically and discrepancies should be pointed out to the child).

General Involvement: Enjoy a traditional folk song together.

Activities: 1) After book has been read, pick out tune and "sing" the book with child; words like "town-o, town-o, town-o" will almost be sung automatically even during the first reading; if you play a musical instrument, accompany your singing. 2) Try to memorize the song so it can be sung wherever you are; traveling in the car, for instance. 3) Substitute other animals and make up your own folk song. 4) Add rhythm instruments (even if only spoons and pots and pans) and add vocal sound effects; record this version. 5) Pantomime actions of the song as you play your tape. 6) Make a "TV roller show" (section off shelf paper attached with tape to towel rollers or wax paper rollers); draw a picture of each event in the song and move the paper as those sequences are heard on the tape.

Yolen, Jane. *All in the Woodland Early: An ABC Book*. Illus: Jane Breskin Zalben. Cleveland: Collins-World, 1979.

The music and the lyrics for this song are by the author. A young fellow and girl go "hunting" all in the woodland early. The animals they find are in alphabetical order, accompanied with beautiful color illustrations. Musical score and lyrics appear at the end.

Topics Covered: Animals in the alphabet; hunting for friends; singing a folksong.

General Involvement: Sing the song; make up new verses.

Activities: 1) Sing the song and take turns singing the refrain. 2) Go on a walk and see what animals you can find. 3) Make an animal alphabet book together with your child. 4) Make up new verses to the song.

Zemach, Margot. *Hush, Little Baby*. New York: E. P. Dutton, 1970.

The well-known lullaby that begins, "Hush, little baby, don't say a word," is presented in illustrations of a Victorian setting.

Topics Covered: Household and other familiar objects.

General Involvement: Help your child to see alternatives—if that . . . , then. . . . This is a simplified way for him to understand cause and effect.

Activities: 1) Sing the song. 2) Sing it a second time adding actions: pulling like a bull, pretending there is a huge diamond on the hand. 3) After the verse is familiar, substitute other words: "Hush, little baby, don't be late, I'm going to buy you a roller skate." 4) Share the book by Harve and Margot Zemach entitled *Mommy, Buy Me A China Doll*, (New York: Farrar, Straus and Giroux, 1966) which is an Ozark Mountain song and bears some resemblance to *Hush, Little Baby* in its sequence.

Poetry

Ciardi, John. *I Met A Man*. Boston: Houghton Mifflin, 1961.

A poetry book designed for beginning readers and containing humorous poems that you both will enjoy.

Topics Covered: Poems beginning with a phrase like "I met a man" and continuing with the different things he might do.

General Involvement: Enjoy reading the poems together.

Activities: 1) Omit the last words of lines and ask your child to fill in the rhyming word or ask your child to read and have you fill in the missing rhyme. 2) Make up and illustrate your own "I Met a Man" poems.

Farber, Norma. *As I Was Crossing Boston Common*. Illus: Arnold Lobel. New York: E. P. Dutton, 1975.
Exceptional children's books often contain something a parent can learn. In this case, a turtle's alphabetic stroll across the Boston Common uncovers a host of real, yet unusual animals: angwantibo, boobook, coypu, desman, entellus, and others.

Topics Covered: The alphabet; uncommon animals; the Boston Common.

General Involvement: Learn about uncommon animals.

Activities: 1) Look up information about rare animals and animals facing extinction. 2) Find out more about the animals mentioned in this book. Start with the key in the back of the book. 3) Visit a local park and observe the animals you see there.

Hopkins, Lee Bennett. *Go To Bed, A Book of Bedtime Poems*. New York: Alfred A. Knopf, 1979.
A compilation of short and delightful poems perfect for bedtime reading.

Topics Covered: Stars; moon; dreams; and many more words and situations associated with getting ready for bed and sleeping.

General Involvement: Enjoy reading these poems at bedtime.

Activities: 1) Memorize one or more of the poems to say together at bedtime as part of your goodnight ritual. 2) Together, write and read your own bedtime poem.

Moore, Lillian. *I Feel The Same Way*. Illus: Beatrice Darwin. New York: Atheneum, 1966.
A delightful collection of easy-to-read poems about the way a young child perceives the environment.

Topics Covered: Rain; ants; bugs; fireflies; sand castles; many others.

General Involvement: Enjoy, enjoy, enjoy the poems!

Activities: 1) Read the poems together; read alternate lines with your child. 2) Tape the poems so they may be listened to at bedtime or at a quiet time during the day. 3) Dramatize the poems: blow dragon smoke; feel your heart go thump; approach corners with a mysterious caution. 4) Try to read the poems often enough so they will "get stuck" in your heads; it can be the delight of both of you to rattle off many of these poems without the book.

Miscellaneous

Cerf, Bennett. *Bennett Cerf's Book of Riddles*. (I Can Read By Myself Beginner Books). New York: Random House, 1960.

Many simply written riddles, such as "What is a bird after he is four days old?" (Answer, "Five days old") are presented with humorous illustrations.

Topics Covered: Simple topics that should match the general concepts of a beginning reader, such as planting and birthdays.

General Involvement: See if your beginning reader can stump you as the riddles are read.

Activities: 1) Together, make up new riddles or list other possible answers for the existing riddles. 2) Compile and illustrate a family riddle book.

Lopshire, Robert. *It's Magic?* New York: Macmillan, 1969.

Tad the Great continuously fools Boris with "foolproof" tricks that you or your child can do using objects found in your home. Clear illustrations will help your child follow each step of the "magic."

Topics Covered: The Take Away Trick; Tough Egg; Knot Magic; Magic Picture Trick, and many others.

General Involvement: Enjoy magic. Perhaps your child will trick *you*!

Activities: 1) Select one or two tricks to do initially; gather the materials needed; first practice the trick with your child in private, then together show the trick to someone; as your child becomes adept, encourage her to do tricks for others without your help. 2) If possible, attend a magic show. 3) Teach your child a magic trick that is not in the book. Your library will have additional sources for home magic.

References

[1] Christina Rossetti, "The Clouds," *Poems, An Early-Start Reader* (New York: Grosset and Dunlap, 1965).

[2] Crosby Bonsall, *The Day I had To Play With My Sister* (New York: Harper & Row, 1972).

[3] Janet Schulman, *The Big Hello* (New York: Greenwillow, 1976).

[4] Pat Hutchins, *Titch* (New York: Macmillan, 1971).

[5] Barbara Seuling, *The Teeny Tiny Woman* (New York: Viking, 1976).

[6] Ann McGovern, *Too Much Noise* (Boston: Houghton Mifflin, 1967).

[7] Kenneth Hoskisson, Thomas M. Sherman and Linda L. Smith. "Assisted Reading and Parent Involvement." *The Reading Teacher*, 27 (April 1974); 710–714.

[8] A. A. Milne, *Winnie-The-Pooh* (New York: E. P. Dutton, 1926).

[9] *Cricket, The Magazine for Children*. Walnut Lane, Boulder, Colorado, 80322.

[10] *National Geographic World*, Department 00877, 17th and M Sts., N.W., Washington, D.C. 20036.

[11] Peter Spier, *Gobble, Growl, Grunt*. (Garden City, N.Y.: Doubleday, 1971).

[12] Peter Spier, *Crash! Bang! Boom!* (Garden City, N.Y.: Doubleday, 1972).

[13] Paul Showers, *The Listening Walk* (New York: Thomas Y. Crowell, 1961).

[14] Anne and Harlow Rockwell, *Thruway*. (New York: Macmillan, 1972).

[15] Marjorie Weinman Sharmat, *Mooch The Messy* (New York: Harper & Row, 1976).

[16] Rosemary Wells, *Noisy Nora*. (New York: Dial Press, 1973).

[17] Franz Brandenberg, *Nice New Neighbors* (New York: Greenwillow, 1977).

[18] Helen Piers, *The Mouse Book* (New York: Franklin Watts, 1966).

[19] Arnold Lobel, *Mouse Soup* (New York: Harper & Row, 1977).

[20] Lee Bennett Hopkins, *Books Are By People, More Books Are By More People* (New York: Citation Press).

[21] Paula Winter, *The Bear and the Fly* (New York: Crown, 1976).

V

Summary and What Next?

In the preceding chapters you have read specific ideas for sharing literature with young children. We have encouraged you to read aloud a variety of good books to your child, beginning with your infant and continuing when she is a wiggly toddler, an active preschooler with lots of other interests, and an independent beginning reader.

We have defined "good literature" for each age level. You will find, however, that a really good book for one age will often be good for another age as well for other reasons. Endearing characters, interesting plots, language play, and beautiful illustrations have universal appeal.

We have stressed the importance of developing good family reading habits and of making your home reading

environment a stimulating one. Supplying your child
with visually appealing books, and later, magazines, and
teaching him to value reading materials and to handle
them carefully, will pay big dividends in terms of his
attitudes toward reading—and also toward school. If a
child grows up in a home where adults read and share
literature, where a quiet time is provided for reading
together that is not in competition with television and
other distractions, the child, too, will learn to love literature.

Parents of young children do not use their public libraries as much as they could. Programs for infants and
toddlers are becoming more common with the recognition that habits begun early are likely to last. In these
days of inflation parents cannot possibly provide their
children with a rich variety of literature without using
the resources of the public library. And since many public libaries now have mail service, libraries are now
within reach of many homes that at one time were re-
mote. The message is clear—develop the family library
habit. You will all enjoy it.

In each chapter dealing with a different age group, we
have talked about reading aloud. Every author who
writes on early childhood reading encourages parents to
read aloud to their children. Most parents realize that
they should read to their children. Some states (Maryland, for example) have even mounted campaigns to encourage parental reading in the home.

Our suggestions go further, however. We advocate
reading aloud to infants as well as older children. We
stress the importance of reading "Sustaining Books"—
longer books, a chapter of which is read each night—and
of continuing to read aloud to children even after they
have learned to read for themselves. Further, we have
provided evidence that the way you read is just as impor-

tant as making a time to read. It is all the discussion surrounding the book and the ways in which you get your child involved in the storyreading that enhance the value of the experience for your child.

The last section of each chapter has presented an annotated booklist of books that parents have enjoyed using with their children. For most titles listed we have suggested ways in which you could involve your child with the book beyond merely reading it aloud. Though we caution against overdoing it, it is these "stretching" activities that make a book special to a child. Many of these activities will also enhance prereading and beginning reading skills.

What Next for Older Children?

If you follow the message of the preceeding chapters, it is not difficult to guess what we would recommend for children who become accomplished readers (usually in the middle grades). *Continue* to provide stimulating reading materials in your home. Subscribe to several children's magazines. *Continue* to make regular visits to the public library and to attend special events there. *Continue* to provide a quiet time daily in which all members of your family will read. *Continue* to read aloud a chapter at a time from more challenging books.

In addition to continuing the practices that have stimulated your child's enthusiastic response to literature, you will want to begin some new activities. A child may be able to read well silently, but need practice in developing good oral reading skills. Now is the time for the older child to read aloud on a regular basis to a younger child—a sibling or a neighbor. Now is the time to tape stories for a nursery school or day care center.

The older child, no longer a beginning reader, needs to develop comprehension and speed. The former can be aided by family book discussions that compare books on a similar topic or works by the same author. Discuss reasons for characterization and plot, and talk about feelings engendered by the book. You can help your child *think* about what he reads. Your family might embark upon a study of some topic where older children can read from a variety of sources for specific information, such as the birds in your neighborhood, or a community problem.

Occasionally see how many pages (or lines or words) each member of the family can read in a specified amount of time. This will give your child periodic help at changing the rate of speed with which she reads.

If you have encouraged your child to enjoy books as a baby and young child, you can be confident that by the time he has learned how to read he will already be "addicted," and a familiar cry in your home will be, when you call your child to dinner, "Just wait till I read one more page—please!" That has been the goal of this book.

APPENDIX A

Children's Magazines

There are not many magazines suitable for the very young child. Three that maintain a high standard of editorial material and exclude junk advertisements are:

Highlights for Children
2300 West Fifth Avenue
Columbus, OH 43216

Inside the Ark
P.O. Box 905-A
Richmond, VA 23207

Humpty Dumpty's Magazine for
Little Children, Subscription
Bergenfield, NJ 07621

Magazines for older children (ages 5–6 and up) include:

Childrens Digest, Subscriptions
Bergenfield, NJ 07621

Children's Playmate
1100 Waterway Blvd., P.O. Box 567-B
Indianapolis, IN 46206

Cricket
Box 100
LaSalle, IL 61301

Ebony Jr.
Johnson Publishing Co.
820 South Michigan Avenue
Chicago, IL 60605

Jack and Jill
1100 Waterway Blvd.
Indianapolis, IN 46206

Kids Magazine
747 Third Avenue
New York, NY 10017

National Geographic World
17th and M Street, N. W.
Washington, D.C. 20036

Ranger Rick's Nature Magazine
National Wildlife Federation
1412 16th Street N.W.
Washington, D.C. 20036

Stone Soup
P.O. Box 83
Santa Cruz, California 95063

Usually publishers will send you a free sample
magazine if you are a prospective subscriber.

APPENDIX *B*

Publishers of Children's Books

Addison-Wesley, Inc.
Reading MA 01867

Atheneum Publishers
122 East 42 Sreet
New York NY 10017

The Bobbs-Merrill Co.
4 West 58 Street
New York NY 10019

Bowmar Publishers
4563 Colorado Boulevard
Los Angeles CA 90039

Brimax Books
347 U Cherry Hinton Road
Cambridge, England CB1 4DH

Collier Books
866 Third Avenue
New York NY 10022

Collins-World
2080 West 117 Street
Cleveland OH 44111

Coward-McCann and Geoghegan
200 Madison Avenue
New York NY 10016

Thomas Y. Crowell
521 Fifth Avenue
New York NY 10017

Crown Publishers
1 Park Avenue
New York NY 10016

Delacorte Press/Dial Press
1 Dag Hammarskjold Plaza
245 East 47 Street
New York NY 10017

Doubleday and Company
245 Park Avenue
New York NY 10017

E. P. Dutton
2 Park Avenue
New York NY 10016

Farrar, Straus and Giroux
19 Union Square West
New York NY 10003

Follett Publishing Co.
1010 West Washington
   Boulevard
Chicago IL 60607

Four Winds Press
Scholastic Book Services
50 West 44 Street
New York NY 10036

Golden Press
Western Publishing
850 Third Avenue
New York NY 10022

Greenwillow Books
105 Madison Avenue
New York NY 10016

Grosset & Dunlap
51 Madison Avenue
New York NY 10010

Harcourt Brace Jovanovich
757 Third Avenue
New York NY 10017

Harper & Row
10 East 53 Street
New York, NY 10022

Holiday House
18 East 53 Street
New York NY 10022

Holt, Rinehart & Winston
383 Madison Avenue
New York NY 10017

Houghton Mifflin Company
1 Beacon Street
Boston MA 02107

Alfred A. Knopf
201 East 50 Street
New York NY 10022

Lippincott Crowell
10 East 53 Street
New York NY 10022

Little, Brown & Company
34 Beacon Street
Boston MA 02106

Lothrop, Lee & Shepard
105 Madison Avenue
New York NY 10016

Ladybird Books Ltd.
P.O. Box 12, Beeches Rd.
Loughborough, Leicestershire
LE11 2NQ, England

The Macmillan Company
866 Third Avenue
New York NY 10022

McGraw-Hill Book Co.
1221 Ave. of the Americas
New York NY 10020

William Morrow
105 Madison Avenue
New York NY 10016

Oxford University Press
200 Madison Avenue
New York NY 10016

Pantheon Books
201 East 50 Street
New York NY 10022

Parents' Magazine Press
52 Vanderbilt Avenue
New York NY 10017

Penguin Books
625 Madison Avenue
New York NY 10022

S. G. Phillips, Inc.
305 West 86 Street
New York NY 10024

Platt & Munk
51 Madison Avenue
New York NY 10010

Prentice-Hall, Inc.
Englewood Cliffs NJ 07632

G. P. Putnam's Sons
200 Madison Avenue
New York NY 10016

Rand McNally & Co.
Box 7600
Chicago IL 60680

Random House, Inc.
201 East 50 Street
New York NY 10022

Scholastic Book Services
50 West 44 Street
New York NY 10036

Charles Scribner's Sons
597 Fifth Avenue
New York NY 10017

Seabury Press
815 Second Avenue
New York NY 10017

The Viking Press
625 Madison Avenue
New York NY 10022

Henry Z. Walck
750 Third Avenue
New York NY 10017

Walker and Company
720 Fifth Avenue
New York NY 10019

Frederick Warne & Co.
101 Fifth Avenue
New York NY 10003

Franklin Watts, Inc.
730 Fifth Avenue
New York NY 10019

John Weatherhill, Inc.
149 Madison Avenue
New York NY 10016

Western Publishing Co.
850 Third Avenue
New York NY 10022

Albert Whitman & Co.
560 West Lake Street
Chicago IL 60606

World Book-Childcraft
   International, Inc.
 501 Merchandise Mart
 Chicago IL 60654

Index of Titles from the Selected Booklists

Index of Authors and Illustrators from the Selected Booklists

Note: Illustrators of books other than their own are marked with an asterisk.